Introduction, interviews and other texts by Hans Lijklema
Edited by Kevin Haworth
Text editing by Kevin Haworth and Ros Horton
Translations by Scriptware (Polish to English and
English to German) and LocTeam (French and Spanish)

Cover and book design by Hans Lijklema
www.lijklema.waw.pl
The cover image was created using the typeface
Takraf 3D (see page 235), designed by Jan Sonntag of
Sonntag Fonts (pages 231-236). www.sonntag.nl

All text in this book has been set in the Anivers typeface
(see page 82), designed by Jos Buivenga of the exljbris
font foundry (pages 81-90). www.exljbris.nl

Free Font Index 1
ISBN 978 90 5768 124 0
The Pepin Press | Agile Rabbit Editions
Amsterdam & Singapore

The Pepin Press BV
P.O. Box 10349
1001 EH Amsterdam
The Netherlands

Tel +31 20 4202021
Fax +31 20 4201152
mail@pepinpress.com
www.pepinpress.com

10 9 8 7 6 5 4 3 2
2014 13 12 11 10 09

Manufactured in Singapore

For Karolina

Hans Lijklema would like to thank:
All the designers and type foundries that have agreed to
participate in this project. Pepin for his support and agree-
ing to publish this book. Kevin for the great cooperation.
And of course Jos for offering to design an *Italic* and **Bold**
weight to accompany his beautiful Anivers typeface, that
I have used throughout this book. (*Man, je bent bijna te
aardig voor deze wereld.*)

Contents

Introduction (EN) 5

Einführung (DE) 7

Introduction (FR) 9

Introducción (ES) 11

CD and font licensing information 13

Information zu CD und Schriftlizenzierung 13

Informations de licence concernant 13
le CD et les fontes

Información sobre el CD y las licencias 13
de las tipografías

Interviews (EN)
  Jos Buivenga – exljbris 15
  Janusz Marian Nowacki 18
  FontStruct 21
  Brode Vosloo 24
  Lopetz – Büro Destruct 27
  Shamrock 30

Interviews (DE) 287

Interviews (FR) 297

Entrevistas (ES) 307

Index 317

Type foundries | Schriftenherausgeber
Fonderies de caractères | Fundiciones
tipográficas
  Astigmatic One Eye 35
  boodas.de 41
  Brain Eaters Font Co. 45
  Brode Vosloo 49
  Bumbayo Font Fabrik 55
  defaulterror 59
  Dieter Steffmann 63
  eightface 75
  exljbris 81
  Fenotype 91
  Flat-it type foundry 103
  Fonthead Design Inc. 111
  Grixel 117
  GUST e-foundry 123
  Igino Marini 127
  Janusz Marian Nowacki 133
  La Tipomatika 145
  Larabie Fonts 149
  Manfred Klein Fonteria 161
  MartinPlus 173
  Misprinted Type 177
  Nick's Fonts 181
  Objets Dart 193
  pizzadude.dk 201
  Reading Type 213
  Rob Meek 219
  Shamfonts 223
  SMeltery 227
  Sonntag Fonts 231
  Typedifferent 237
  Typodermic Fonts 249
  Vic Fieger 257
  VTKS Design 263
  WC Fonts 275
  Yanone 283

Technology has drastically changed the graphics industry over the last couple of decades. Almost everything has gone digital. One of the things that has been affected most is the production of typefaces: within a time period of 50 years we have gone from metal type, to photo setting, to computer-based font software. Many famous type foundries have merged, closed their doors or have even been bought by small digital type foundries. In the past, it was impossible for an individual to design a typeface, produce it and distribute it – the costs involved were too great. Programs like Fontographer gave designers the tools to produce fonts in their own homes and the Internet gave them the means to distribute their work. Thanks to the Internet, individuals and large type foundries have the same access to a hungry international audience of designers who are continually looking for new typefaces to use in their work. Thanks to these changes, an overwhelming number of new typefaces have been made available during the last two decades – so many, that some designers have decided to make part or whole collections of fonts available for free. Some release free fonts because they want to attract visitors to their websites; others don't see the point in selling them because there are already so many fonts

Self-promotional A3 poster for the boodas.de font collection (see page 41). © 2008 Boris Schandert | boodas.de

available. Some create fonts as a hobby or as therapy. There are also those who create a typeface but don't feel like completing the character set, which is necessary for commercial sales. And there are, of course, designers who believe in the democracy and community spirit of the Internet and make their work available in the public domain.

URLs change, sites disappear and typeface designers move on to do other things with their lives. The Internet is ever changing, so with this book I hope to document the free fonts that are being created at the moment and show what has been done in the past.

A lot of us select and buy our fonts through the Internet, and very often we see them for the first time in print after we have used them for a specific design project. Fewer and fewer letterproofs are being published by commercial foundries and free fonts are, of course, never shown in catalogues. Hopefully this book will fill the gap.

With this book, I also want to showcase the work of the designers/foundries and give them credit and appreciation for the work they do. I think that many people who download free fonts from the Internet know little about – or simply are not interested in – the font designers. I sat down with some of the people who create free fonts to talk about their work and their reasons for sharing their fonts with all of us. You can read the resulting interviews on the following pages.

I decided to include only 'real' free fonts in this book. I find that the term 'free font' as used on the Internet is often confusing or misleading. Some fonts that are called 'free' still require the end user to buy a licence for commercial use. For me, the issue is not whether a designer/foundry wants to restrict commercial use; they have every right to decide how their fonts can be used. But I think the title 'free' is being misused. Fonts with restrictions should be called "shareware" or "free for personal (or non-commercial) use". All fonts in this book are free for personal and commercial use. However, they are not in the Public Domain – restrictions do apply. Please read the End User Licence Agreement (EULA) documents that are included for each font before using any font.

I hope you enjoy the book and that it will awaken your interest in the creators of these wonderful typefaces. I encourage you to visit their sites to check out their other fonts and support them by purchasing one of their commercial fonts or by sending them a message to let them know you appreciate their work. Hopefully they will be encouraged to create more great fonts.

Hans Lijklema

Im Laufe der letzten Jahrzehnte hat Technologie die Grafikindustrie drastisch verändert. Nahezu alles ist jetzt digital. Ein Bereich, in dem sich diese Veränderung am stärksten ausgeprägt had, ist das Produzieren von Schriftarten. Innerhalb einer Zeitspanne von 50 Jahren haben wir eine Entwicklung erlebt, die von Lettern aus Metall über Fotosatz bis zu computerbasierter Fontsoftware verlaufen ist. Viele berühmte Schriftenherausgeber sind fusioniert, haben aufgegeben oder wurden von kleineren digitalen Herausgebern aufgekauft. In der Vergangenheit war es für eine einzelne Person unmöglich, eine Schriftart zu entwerfen, produzieren und zu vertreiben – die Kosten waren dafür viel zu hoch. Programme wie Fontographer gaben Gestaltern die Werkzeuge, Schriftarten zuhause zu produzieren und das Internet gab ihnen die Möglichkeit, ihre Arbeit zu veröffentlichen. Dank dem Internet haben sowohl Einzelpersonen als auch große Schriftenherausgeber den gleichen Zugang auf einen hungrigen internationalen Kreis von Designern, die ununterbrochen nach neuen Schriftarten suchen, die sie in ihrer Arbeit verwenden können.

Aufgrund dieser Veränderungen wurde in den letzten zwei Jahrzehnten eine Vielzahl von neuen Schriftarten verfügbar – so viele, dass manche Designer die Entscheidung getroffen haben, einen Teil oder sogar ganze Sammlungen von Schriften gratis verfügbar zu machen. Manche veröffentlichen kostenlose Schriften, um Besucher zu ihren Websites zu locken, andere sehen den Sinn des Verkaufs nicht ein, da es schon so viele Fonts gibt. Manche erstellen Schriften als ein Hobby oder gar als Therapie. Es gibt ebenfalls welche, die eine Schriftart erstellen, aber den Zeichensatz nicht vervollständigen möchten, der für einen kommerzi-

Promotional image for the WC Wunderbach Mix typeface (see page 281). © 2008 WC Fonts

ellen Verkauf notwendig wäre. Und natürlich gibt es Designer, die an Demokratie im Internet glauben und ihre Arbeit für jeden zugänglich machen möchten.

URLs ändern sich, Websites verschwinden und Designer von Schriftarten widmen sich anderen Themen. Das Internet ändert sich immerzu; daher versuche ich mit diesem Buch, die kostenlosen Fonts zu dokumentieren, die zurzeit gestaltet werden und zu zeigen, was in der Vergangenheit geschaffen wurde.

Viele von uns wählen und beziehen unsere Schriften über das Internet und wir sehen sie oftmals das erste Mal in Druckform, nachdem die Fonts für ein bestimmtes Designprojekt verwendet wurden. Kommerzielle Schriftenherausgeber geben immer weniger Schriftmuster heraus und kostenlose Fonts werden natürlich nie in Katalogen präsentiert. Hoffentlich kann dieses Buch diese Lücke füllen.

Mit diesem Buch möchte ich ebenfalls die Arbeit von Designer und Schriftherausgebern vorstellen und sie für diese Arbeit anerkennen. Ich denke, dass viele Personen, die kostenlose Schriften aus dem Internet herunterladen, wenig über die Schriftdesigner wissen — oder einfach nicht daran interessiert sind. Ich habe mich mit einer Reihe von Personen, die kostenlose Schriften kreieren, zusammengesetzt, über ihre Arbeit gesprochen und sie über die Gründe befragt, weshalb sie ihre Fonts mit uns allen teilen möchten. Sie können diese Interviews auf den folgenden Seiten lesen.

Ich habe mich entschieden, nur wirklich „kostenlose" Schriften in diesem Buch aufzunehmen. Ich finde den Begriff „kostenlose Fonts", wie dieser auf dem Internet verwendet wird, oftmals verwirrend und irreführend. Manche

Schriften werden als „kostenlos" bezeichnet, obwohl der Endbenutzer dennoch eine Lizenz für kommerziellen Gebrauch kaufen muss. Es ist für mich nicht die Frage, ob ein Designer oder Herausgeber die kommerzielle Verwendung beschränken will; sie haben schließlich jedes Recht, zu entscheiden wie ihre Fonts verwendet werden. Aber ich denke, dass der Begriff „kostenlos" dabei in einer irreleitenden Art und Weise verwendet wird. Fonts mit Einschränkungen sollten als „Shareware" oder „kostenlos für private (nicht kommerzielle) Verwendung" beschrieben werden. Die Fonts in diesem Buch sind kostenlos für sowohl private als auch kommerzielle Zwecke. Sie befinden sich jedoch nicht im öffentlichem Besitz — einige Einschränken gelten. Bitte lesen Sie die Dokumente zur Endbenutzer-Lizenzvereinbarung (EULA), die für jeden einzelnen Font beigeschlossen sind, vor Verwendung der betreffenden Schrift.

Ich hoffe, dass Sie Gefallen an diesem Buch finden und es Ihr Interesse an den Designern dieser wundervollen Schriftarten weckt. Ich möchte Sie ermutigen, die zahlreichen Websites zu besuchen, die anderen Schriften zu entdecken und die Erzeuger mit dem Kauf ihrer kommerziellen Fonts zu unterstützen. Oder ihnen eine E-Mail zu schicken, in der Sie ihre Arbeit anerkennen. Hoffentlich werden die Designer dazu angeregt, noch weitere phantastische Schriften zu schaffen.

Hans Lijklema

L'industrie graphique a connu des changements radicaux au cours des deux dernières
décennies. Tout ou presque est devenu
numérique. L'une des choses qui a le plus
changé est la production des caractères :
sur une période de cinquante ans, nous
sommes passés des caractères en plomb aux
logiciels de création de polices de caractères,
en passant par la photocomposition. De
nombreuses fonderies de caractères ont dû
fusionner ou fermer, ou bien ont même été
rachetées par de petites sociétés de création
de fontes numériques.

Autrefois, il était impossible à une personne
seule de dessiner, de produire et de distribuer
un type de caractères : les coûts occasionnés
étaient trop élevés. Des logiciels tels que
Fontographer ont fourni aux graphistes les
outils nécessaires pour créer eux-mêmes leurs
fontes et Internet leur a donné la possibilité
de les distribuer. Grâce à Internet, les graphistes du monde entier, sans cesse à la
recherche de nouveaux types de caractères
pour leur travail, peuvent accéder aussi bien
aux fontes créées par un individu seul que par
une grande fonderie de caractères.

Grâce à ces changements, une quantité
impressionnante de nouveaux types de caractères a vu le jour au cours des deux dernières
décennies, au point que certains créateurs
ont décidé de mettre gratuitement une partie
ou la totalité de leur collection à la disposition des utilisateurs. Certains le font parce
qu'ils souhaitent attirer des visiteurs sur leur
site Web, d'autres parce qu'ils ne voient pas
l'intérêt de les vendre, vu la très grande quantité de fontes déjà disponibles. Pour certains,
la création de fontes est un passe-temps ou

Media Pigeons: the more letters you type the more interesting the result will be (see page 176). © 2008 Martin Wenzel

une thérapie. Il y a aussi ceux qui créent un type de caractères mais qui n'ont pas envie de terminer la série complète, ce qui est nécessaire en vue d'une commercialisation. Et il existe, bien sûr, des créateurs qui croient à la démocratie et l'esprit de communauté d'Internet et qui rendent leur travail disponible sur le domaine public.

Les adresses Web changent, les sites disparaissent et, parfois, les créateurs décident de faire autre chose de leur vie. Internet connaît des changements perpétuels et ce livre a pour objectif de fournir un aperçu des fontes gratuites qui ont été crées récemment et de montrer ce qui a été fait auparavant.

Beaucoup de graphistes choisissent et achètent leurs fontes sur Internet et ne voient le résultat imprimé pour la première fois qu'après avoir utilisé ces fontes pour un projet particulier. Les fonderies commerciales publient de moins en moins souvent de catalogues de fontes et, bien sûr, les fontes libres ne sont jamais présentées dans des catalogues. J'espère que ce livre aidera à combler un tel manque.

J'ai également voulu présenter dans ce livre le travail des créateurs individuels et des fonderies, leur rendre l'honneur qu'ils méritent et les remercier de leur travail. Il me semble que la plupart des personnes qui téléchargent des fontes libres sur Internet ne connaissent pratiquement rien, ou ne s'intéressent tout simplement pas, à leurs créateurs. J'ai rencontré certains créateurs de fontes libres pour parler de leur travail et des raisons pour lesquelles ils ont décidé de mettre gratuitement leurs fontes à la disposition du public. Vous trouverez les entrevues correspondantes dans les pages qui suivent.

Dans ce livre, j'ai décidé de ne présenter que des fontes véritablement gratuites. Je trouve que le terme « fonte libre » tel qu'il est utilisé sur Internet est souvent déroutant ou trompeur. Pour certaines fontes soi-disant « libres », l'utilisateur doit néanmoins acheter une licence en cas d'utilisation commerciale. La question pour moi n'est pas de juger la décision d'un créateur individuel ou d'une fonderie de restreindre l'utilisation commerciale. Chacun a le droit de décider des conditions d'utilisation de ses fontes. Mais dans ce cas, je pense que le terme « libre » est mensonger. Les fontes assujetties à des restrictions devraient être qualifiées de fontes « contributives » ou « libres pour usage personnel (ou non-commerciales) ». Toutes les fontes présentées dans ce livre sont libres pour une utilisation personnelle ou commerciale. Cependant, elles n'appartiennent pas au domaine public et des restrictions s'appliquent. Avant d'utiliser une fonte, veuillez lire le contrat de licence d'utilisateur final (CLU) fourni avec chaque fonte.

J'espère que vous apprécierez ce livre et qu'il éveillera votre intérêt pour les créateurs de ces fontes merveilleuses. Je vous encourage à visiter leur site Web pour découvrir d'autres fontes de ces créateurs, ainsi qu'à les aider en achetant une de leurs fontes commerciales ou en leur envoyant un message pour leur faire savoir que vous appréciez leur travail. Avec un peu de chance, cela les encouragera à créer de nouvelles fontes extraordinaires.

Hans Lijklema

La tecnología ha cambiado la industria gráfica de arriba abajo en el último par de décadas. En la actualidad, prácticamente todo se hace con medios digitales. Uno de los aspectos que más se ha visto afectado por esta transformación es la producción de tipografías: en un lapso de cincuenta años hemos pasado de los tipos de metal a la fotocomposición y el software de diseño de fuentes. Como consecuencia, muchas fundiciones tipográficas conocidas se han fusionado, han cerrado sus puertas o las han adquirido pequeñas fundiciones tipográficas digitales.

En el pasado era impensable que una sola persona diseñara, produjera y distribuyera una tipografía, pues el coste de todo ello era demasiado elevado. Programas como Fontographer pusieron a disposición de los tipógrafos las herramientas para crear fuentes en sus propios hogares, e Internet les proporcionó los medios para distribuir su trabajo. Gracias a la Red, todos, ya sean creadores individuales o grandes fundiciones tipográficas, disfrutan de idéntico acceso a un público internacional de diseñadores ávidos de nuevas familias tipográficas para usar en sus trabajos. Esta renovación del sector ha propiciado la proliferación de gran cantidad de tipografías nuevas en las dos últimas décadas; tantas que algunos diseñadores han decidido distribuir parcial o íntegramente sus colecciones de forma gratuita. Algunos lanzan al mercado fuentes gratuitas con el objetivo de atraer visitantes a sus sitios web, mientras

Opening page of the SMeltery type foundry website (see page 227). © 2008 Jack Usine | SMeltery

que otros sencillamente no le encuentran sentido a venderlas debido a la variedad existente. Los hay que incluso crean fuentes por diversión o a modo de terapia. Otros esbozan las tipografías pero no se detienen a completar todo el juego de caracteres, algo imprescindible para su comercialización. Y, por supuesto, también hay diseñadores que creen en el espíritu democrático y comunitario de Internet y ponen sus creaciones a disposición del dominio público.

Las URL cambian, los sitios web desaparecen y los tipógrafos dedican sus vidas a otros menesteres. Internet es un medio sumido en una metamorfosis perpetua, de modo que mi objetivo en este libro es ceñirme a documentar las fuentes gratuitas que se están creando en este preciso instante y dar cuenta de lo que ha acontecido en el pasado.

Muchos de nosotros seleccionamos y compramos fuentes a través de Internet, y con frecuencia las vemos impresas por primera vez después de aplicarlas a un proyecto de diseño específico. Las fundiciones tipográficas comerciales cada vez publican menos borradores y, lógicamente, no existen catálogos de fuentes gratuitas. Este libro nace con el objetivo de llenar ese vacío.

Este volumen surge también de la voluntad de mostrar el trabajo de los diseñadores y las fundiciones, reconocerles su mérito y felicitarles por sus logros. Creo que muchas personas que se descargan fuentes gratuitas de Internet apenas saben nada de los diseñadores que las crean o, sencillamente, no sienten interés alguno por ellos. Con el fin de conocer más de cerca su trabajo y sus motivos para compartir sus creaciones con todos nosotros

conversé un rato con algunos diseñadores de fuentes gratuitas. En las páginas siguientes se recogen las entrevistas que mantuvimos.

En este libro he optado por incluir exclusivamente tipografías «realmente» gratuitas. Opino que el término «fuente gratuita» (free font) tal como se utiliza en Internet resulta a menudo confuso y puede inducir a error. Algunas tipografías denominadas «gratuitas» exigen al usuario final que adquiera una licencia para su uso comercial. Me parece perfectamente comprensible que un diseñador o una fundición quieran restringir su uso comercial; tienen derecho a decidir cómo se utilizan, pero creo que el adjetivo «gratuito» está mal empleado en este caso. Las tipografías con restricciones deberían llamarse «shareware» o «gratuitas para uso personal (o no comercial)». Todas las tipografías incluidas en este libro pueden emplearse gratuitamente con fines personales y comerciales. Ahora bien, no son de dominio público, sino que existen algunas restricciones. No olvide leer los contratos de licencia para usuarios finales (EULA) que se incluyen con cada fuente antes de utilizarla.

Espero que disfrute del libro y que despierte su interés por los creadores de estas fabulosas tipografías. Le animo a visitar sus páginas web para conocer otras de sus creaciones, colaborar con ellos adquiriendo una de sus familias tipográficas comerciales o enviarles un mensaje para hacerles saber que aprecia su trabajo. Con un poco de suerte, eso los estimulará a concebir nuevas tipografías magníficas.

Hans Lijklema

CD and font licensing

The free fonts included on the CD-ROM accompanying this book are licensed by their respective designers/foundries for use solely by the owner of this book. Although all free fonts included with this book are licensed for personal and commercial use, you may only use the fonts in accordance with the terms set forth in the respective End User Licence Agreements (EULAs). Please consult the appropriate EULA and/or 'read me' files, included with each font on the CD-ROM, before using any font.

The Pepin Press, the author and the font designers are not liable for any damage resulting from the use of the CD-ROM, font software or any accompanying documentation. Please contact the individual designers/foundries for additional information on licensing.

Contrat de licence concernant le CD et les fontes

Les fontes libres contenues dans le CD-ROM accompagnant le livre font l'objet d'une licence de la part de leur créateur ou fonderie respectif qui restreint leur utilisation au propriétaire de ce livre exclusivement. Bien que toutes les fontes libres fournies avec ce livre bénéficient d'une licence pour usage personnel et commercial, leur utilisation doit respecter les conditions stipulées dans les contrats de licence d'utilisateur final (CLU) respectifs. Avant d'utiliser une fonte, veuillez consulter le CLU et/ou le fichier « read-me » (lisez-moi) accompagnant chaque fonte contenue sur le CD-ROM.

L'éditeur Pepin Press, l'auteur et les créateurs de fontes ne peuvent être tenus responsables des dommages pouvant résulter de l'utilisation du CD-ROM, du logiciel de fontes ou de la documentation qui les accompagne. Pour de plus amples informations sur les licences, veuillez contacter les créateurs individuels ou les fonderies respectives.

CD und Schriftlizenzierung

Die kostenlosen Schriften auf der beiliegenden CD-ROM werden von ihren betreffenden Designern/Herausgebern ausschließlich für den Gebrauch durch den Eigentümer dieses Buches lizenziert. Obwohl alle kostenlosen Schriften, die diesem Buch beiliegen, für privaten und kommerziellen Gebrauch lizenziert sind, dürfen Sie die Fonts nur zu den Bedingungen, die in der betreffenden Endbenutzer-Lizenzvereinbarung (EULA) festgelegt wurden, verwenden. Bitte ziehen Sie die betreffende EULA bzw. die „Lies mich" (read me) Datei zu Rate, die jeder Schrift auf der CD-ROM beiliegt, bevor Sie einen Font verwenden.

Pepin Press, der Autor und die Schriftdesigner haften nicht für Schäden, die aufgrund der Verwendung der CD-ROM, Fontsoftware oder jeglicher beiliegender Dokumentierung auftreten. Bitte kontaktieren Sie die einzelnen Designer/Schriftenherausgeber für zusätzliche Information über Lizenzierung.

CD y licencias de uso de las tipografías

Las tipografías gratuitas incluidas en el CD-ROM que se adjunta son propiedad de sus respectivos diseñadores/fundiciones y se licencian para uso en exclusiva del propietario de este libro. Pese a que todas las fuentes gratuitas incluidas en este volumen se ceden con licencia tanto para uso personal como comercial, deben usarse con acuerdo a los términos y condiciones establecidos en los contratos de licencia para usuarios finales (EULA) correspondientes. Consulte el EULA pertinente y/o los archivos «read me» (léame) incluidos con cada tipografía en el CD-ROM adjunto antes de utilizarla.

The Pepin Press, el autor y los diseñadores tipográficos quedan exentos de toda responsabilidad por cualquier posible daño derivado del uso del CD-ROM, el software de creación tipográfica o la documentación adjunta. Contacte con los diseñadores o las fundiciones correspondientes si precisa información adicional acerca de los términos de la licencia.

Jos Buivenga – exljbris

Jos Buivenga has been making a name for himself in the last couple of years as a new talent in the world of type design. First, people were in awe of the beautiful free fonts he created and now his first commercial typeface, Museo, is topping the bestseller list of MyFonts. When I decided to set the text of this book in his typeface Anivers, Jos generously offered to finish Anivers Italic and Bold, to broaden the typographic pallet. It is time to get to know this Dutchman a little better.

Your fonts are seen as some of the best free fonts available. They are as good as many commercial typefaces out there and they also contain the same extensive character sets. Why give them away for free?

JB: There was no plan when I made my first typeface, Delicious. I was just fascinated by how it would be to set a text with your own typeface. Since I didn't study type design, the real challenge was to discover all the traps and find proper solutions to come up with a reasonable looking, working font of my

Pages from Jos Buivenga's sketchbook. © 2008 Jos Buivenga | exljbris

own: Delicious. Selling it never crossed my mind … it just felt great when people liked it or wanted to use it. It was only after ten years that I decided to make another font. Fontin still felt like a typographic exploration, which I preferred to share with people rather than selling it to them. Shortly after I finished Fontin, my fonts got listed at Vitaly Friedman's '25 Best Free Quality Fonts' and that's when things really took off. Many people got to know me and my free fonts and the responses were heartwarming — so much so that with every new font I made, I decided to give it away for free.

With Museo and the new version of your Anivers typeface you decided to take a different approach. Some of the weights of the fonts are available as a free download and the other weights you can purchase for a small fee. What brought about the change?
JB: I've worked five days a week for about 12 years. I just wanted more time for designing type so last year, when I got the opportunity to switch jobs and work a day less per week, I was very glad. I wanted to offer pay-fonts so that I could get some financial compensation for that day.

Can you describe the process you go through when you design a typeface?
JB: I sketch a lot. Most of the sketches I can't use, but that doesn't matter, because I really like doing it. Often I use drafts as a starting point for a new typeface, but the real process always takes place on screen. I always start with some lower-case glyphs (a, c, e, f, g, h, i, n, s and v) to get a feel of the new face. If

these are to my liking I work out the rest of the lower case and often, in between, I do the capitals H and O to get a global idea of how everything will fit together. If I also plan on making a bold and italic, I do some quick and dirty preliminary tests to see if the regular may need changes to ensure that all weights and styles work. Usually I roughly determine the sidebearings when working on each glyph and do several adjustment rounds until the spacing is finished. Then it's time to kern and further test the typeface in different situations. After all that is done, I generate the final beta for compatibility testing on different platforms and applications. When everything is as it should be, I finally can release the new typeface.

What are your plans for the future?
JB: I'm currently working on Museo Sans to accompany Museo. Then there's Calluna, my first serious attempt to do a text face. Last, but not least: DeliciousX and Fontin Serif still wait to be finished and I have to update Fontin (Semi) and Fontin Sans with extended language support. Often a new idea comes along (like Calluna when I was working on Museo) and I take a 'break' to investigate if it's worth continuing. It always comes as a natural thing and I never have to bother about what I'm going to do next. Sometimes I wish there were three of me to get all the things done that I want to do.

Oposite, top: Jos Buivenga's Anivers typeface in progress. Bottom: pages from the Museo letterproof.
all images © 2008 Jos Buivenga | exljbris

MUSEO... it all started with my love for U

TROTZKOPF
Quadrillion
MUSEO
typógraphy!
LEGION

Janusz Marian Nowacki

For a long time I was looking for a digital version of my favorite Polish metal type Antykwa Półtawskiego. After asking around I found out that an organisation called GUST (the Polish users' group of the free typesetting software called TeX) offered it on their site for free. The quality was very good and on the same site were several other carefully crafted revivals of Polish metal typefaces. They all had one thing in common: Janusz Marian Nowacki.

How did you get the idea to digitise classic Polish typefaces?
JMN: The first computer appeared on my desk in 1990 – it coincided with the change in the political system in Poland. I was 40 then and that is how I started my adventure with computers. Up until then I didn't know anything at all about them. I needed to learn the very basics. I am a journalist by profession. I used to spend quite a lot of time in the printing house supervising the typesetting of the newspaper I worked for before martial law was imposed (in 1981). At that time, I became familiar with the basics of typography and I met experienced typesetters. I also learned about Polish metal typefaces. When I changed to the computer, I was typographically disappointed. Computer-aided typesetting seemed

less complicated and offered new opportunities. However, I couldn't use my favourite Polish typefaces. The only typefaces available were Times, Helvetica and Courier. If you wanted something else, you had two options: either buy the thing or create it yourself. As there were no Polish typefaces for sale, I had to choose the latter.

Can you tell me how you started to design typefaces?
JMN: My early attempts to design typefaces were so primitive and unsuccessful that I'd better not mention them. I guess I began working seriously on the first version of Antykwa Toruńska in 1994. The drawings of particular letters were created in CorelDraw and then I imported them into Fontographer. The results were acceptable, however as it later turned out, they left much to be desired. Typefaces are not only beautiful letter shapes, they also contain a lot of technical issues that a designer does not need to concern himself with.

Oposite, top left: metal type Antykwa Toruńska.
photo © 2005 Janusz Marian Nowacki
Letterproof details of Antykwa Toruńska (top right) and Antykwa Półtawskiego (bottom), from the catalogue of the Warszawska Odlewnia Czcionek (Warsaw Typeface Foundry).

ANTYKWA PÓŁTAWSKIEGO PÓŁGRUBA

Drukarstwo, sztuka drukarska, pierwotnie sztuka odbijania pisma przy pomocy ruchomych czcionek, opiera się na wynalazku odlewnictwa czcionek. W Europie sztukę drukowania wynaleziono w połowie XV wieku. Drukarstwo, sztuka
DRUKARSTWO, SZTUKA DRUKARSKA, PIERWOTNIE SZTUKA ODBIJANIA PISMA PRZY POMOCY RUCHOMYCH 1234567 — 6 p.

Drukarstwo, sztuka drukarska, pierwotnie sztuka odbijania pisma przy pomocy ruchomych
czcionek, opiera się na wynalazku odlewnictwa czcionek. W Europie sztukę drukowania 890
DRUKARSTWO, SZTUKA DRUKARSKA, PIERWOTNIE SZTUKA ODBIJANIA PISMA PRZY 789 — 8 p.

Drukarstwo, sztuka drukarska, pierwotnie sztuka odbijania pisma przy 1023
DRUKARSTWO, SZTUKA DRUKARSKA, PIERWOTNIE SZTUKA ODBIJANIA — 10 p.

Drukarstwo, sztuka drukarska, pierwotnie sztuka odbijania pisma
DRUKARSTWO, SZTUKA DRUKARSKA, PIERWOTNIE SZTUKA 67 — 12 p.

Drukarstwo, sztuka drukarska, pierwotnie sztuka odbijania
DRUKARSTWO, SZTUKA DRUKARSKA, PIERWOTNIE 458 — 16 p.

Drukarstwo, sztuka drukarska, PIERWOTNIE — 20 p.

Drukarstwo sztuka DRUKARSKA 1738459 — 24 p.

Drukarstwo sztuka DRUKARSKA 2 — 28 p.

Drukarstwo SZTUKA DRUK

ODLEWNIA CZCIONEK · WARSZAWA · REJTANA 16

What did you use as material for the digitisation? I know that for the Antykwa Toruńska typeface you had access to the original designs.
JMN: The source for the first version was a catalogue of the Warszawska Odlewnia Czcionek (Warsaw Typeface Foundry). Having prepared the draft version of Antykwa Toruńska, I paid a visit to its creator, Zygfryd Gardzielewski, with a huge stack of print-outs. We thoroughly discussed every letter and I revised my ideas. Zygfryd Gardzielewski accepted the idea of producing fonts. He knew it was the only way to keep his work alive since changes in printing technologies meant that only computer readable formats would survive. As a goodbye gift, he gave me all the design materials that he still possessed. So I had to start again, but this time with a better source of graphic materials. I continued consulting with Zygfryd Gardzielewski until his death in 2001. After his death, I had to solve design problems on my own.

You decided to expand the amount of glyphs for the typefaces far beyond the original amount of languages they covered...
JMN: The original typefaces of Antykwa Toruńska only allowed for typesetting texts in a few Latin languages: Polish, German, French and English. There were no other languages needed in Poland at the time of their creation in the 1950s. In the first publicised version, I added some accented letters and different characters necessary for computer typesetting that were not included in the metal typeface. The basic format for the fonts was PostScript Type1, which allowed for only 256 characters.

I was able to do more with the typeface after the appearance of the new OpenType format and I started designing characters that Zygfryd Gardzielewski did not deal with. I created Greek and Cyrillic letters, mathematical symbols and a set of Latin letters that made it possible to typeset texts even in very exotic languages, such as Vietnamese or Navajo. Of course, it wasn't easy at all, as I am not a professional designer. The users can judge my work for themselves.

Seeing the huge amount of time that must have gone in to these projects, why did you decide to give them away for free?
JMN: Had I known how difficult it was to create fonts and how many technological traps there were, I probably wouldn't have even started. I have, however, managed to overcome problems that have arisen and that has been very satisfying. I mainly deal with fonts designed by Poles. We, as a nation, don't seem to have a talent for promoting ourselves and this makes it difficult for us to bring our products to the world, so I decided not to charge for the fonts. This way they may become more popular. I think the Polish typefaces are a part of the world's cultural heritage and I'd like them to be used by anybody who is interested in them.

FontStruct

At the beginning of 2008, a new font editing software was launched in the form of a website. FontStruct, as this nifty little piece of programming is called, has taken the type and design community by storm. It's free to use and the makers encourage users to share the fonts they create. I just had to find out more, so I talked to its creator, Rob Meek, and sponsor, Stephen Coles, who is Type Director of FontShop International.

Where did the original idea for the FontStuct program come from?

RM: FontStruct developed out of a long-standing fascination with modular fonts. Modular fonts are fun and relatively simple to build, ideal for someone who is interested in playing with systems and within limits. And also, I think, they are a good starting point for someone getting into typographic design. FontStruct was conceived as a tool for developing such fonts. It was designed to be simple

FontStruct font gallery with downloadable free fonts. © 2008 FontShop | Rob Meek

and non-technical. It also shares a heritage with my MEEK Typographic Synthesizers – a series of accessible font-designing toys. The MEEK Typographic Synthesizers are fun, esoteric exercises. With FontStruct I wanted to try and develop something that might be of use and interest to a wider audience.

How did FontShop get involved in the development of FontStruct?
SC: FontShop and Rob Meek have had a close working relationship for a long time, adding various enhancements to FontShop.com. Rob approached us with the FontStruct concept and asked us to sponsor and co-produce the site.

Was your original idea also to make it available as a website?
RM: Yes. I think fonts are especially well suited to the new era of online creation and sharing. The relatively small file sizes and the clearly structured creative space lend themselves to browser-based editing. I hope that FontStruct may become a kind of mini-Flickr/ Picnik for the world of modular fonts.

What do you see as the underlying purpose of FontStruct?
SC: There is no better way to gain appreciation for type and the skills required in type design than to try one's hand at the craft. This is why drawing letters is often a part of college-level typography and graphic design courses. FontStruct is part of FontShop's mission to improve awareness of type in general and to raise the perceived value of well-crafted digital typefaces. Creating and sharing

type is a great way to advance this goal and free access is essential to achieving an open and thriving community.
RM: Personally, I hope it is a fun introduction to the pleasure of typographic creation for novices, and a playground for more experienced disciples of the modular font.

Aren't you creating competition for the modular typefaces that you are selling yourself, by encouraging the users of FontStruct to make their fonts available for free?
SC: The FontStructor (the editor within FontStruct) gives the user a surprising level of flexibility, as you can see by the fonts currently in the Gallery. So, yes, allowing free downloads could be seen as a gamble for a font retailer. However, the limitations of the grid don't really allow for the creation of professional-level typefaces. In the end, with FontStruct we are cultivating a global community of type enthusiasts, which will only benefit FontShop, and the industry as a whole.

Rob, you also made a couple of fonts with FontStruct, which are shown in this book. Is your passion for designing fonts or rather for creating the tools that can assist others in doing that?
RM: Definitely the latter. The fact that I have experience as a designer and typographic dabbler, as well as a developer, definitely helped the project, but I am very much in awe of people with genuine typographic passion. Seeing some of the amazing things that others have done with the tool is a great reward for me.

Try it yourself: **fontstruct.fontshop.com**

22

FontStruct editor (top) and preview mode (bottom). images © 2008 FontShop | Rob Meek

Brode Vosloo

Brode Vosloo attained notoriety because of his fonts which try to capture the real African spirit. They are nothing like the stereotypical fonts used by tourist organisations to represent this continent. His inspiration was taken directly from the lettering on the streets. His now defunct type foundry, The Sacred Nipple, received a lot of attention and Vosloo even produced some fonts for Carlos Segura's American cult foundry T.26. And then it all went quiet.

Most of your fonts have been released as free fonts. Why did you initially decide to do that instead of publishing them as pay-fonts?
BV: Although I studied graphic design at one of the most reputable design institutions in Southern Africa, I didn't have the opportunity to study with any skilled typographers or masters of font software programs like Fontographer. I pretty much had to teach myself everything I could about typography and the software used to produce functional fonts. The first fonts I created were experimental endeavours into the world of typography and I honestly didn't feel that they were worth charging anyone money for. As I continued along my typographic journey I realised the need for more uniquely African typefaces – faces that really echoed the grittiness and

energy of the African streets, faces that stood apart from those tacky tourist fonts that were currently being used to represent Africa. And so free fonts like iAlfabhethi, iZulu, Mr CV Joint, Pleine Str., Rural and Star Salon were born. With the guidance of Carlos Segura I then went on to create fully functional pay-fonts, with complete character sets, like the Shoe Repairs and Freeline collections and the pi font Afrodisiac. These fonts are currently released through Segura's T.26 font foundry.

Why did you stop creating free fonts?
BV: In the late nineties it seemed like everyone with a computer and some font creation software was a typographer. There were, and probably still are, many free fonts out there. Often these fonts are just re-interpretations of fonts created in the mid nineties by other designers. I began to feel that anything given away for free through the Internet had no value. After releasing my Shoe Repairs font I knew, first hand, the pain and pleasure that accompanies the arduous task of designing a complete and functional font, and I felt sad to see people choosing free fonts over fonts

Oposite, top: spread to promote Brode Vosloo's Shoe Repairs font family in i-jusi magazine. Bottom: screen grab from Brode Vosloo's The Sacred Nipple type foundry website (now defunct). all images © 2008 Brode Vosloo

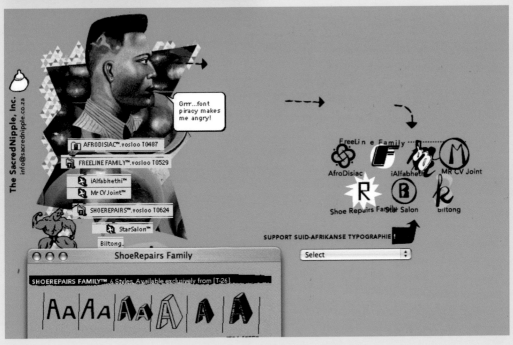

created by skilled typographers. Even the simplest of fonts requires some forethought and elbow grease, two facets of font design which I certainly feel are worth some financial remuneration. Don't get me wrong, though, I'm not all doom and gloom about releasing free fonts. I do believe that the computer has put font creation in the hands of the common designer and this has afforded the opportunity for some amazing ideas to come to life. Free fonts have certainly breathed new life into a craft that was previously reserved for an elite few. I guess that good fonts, much like good cream, will always rise to the top.

It has been a long time since your last type-face. Has there been a change of focus in your work?

BV: It's certainly been some time since I last released a new typeface. This is largely because I moved out of the pure graphic design work environment and into other areas like motion design and fashion design. I have still been laying down some ideas for new faces and been using them in my work. I now work in the action sports industry for a brand whose roots originally lay in motocross and is now also firmly entrenched in the BMX, surf and wakeboard lifestyles. I am their market-ing manager and the job is the ideal blend between my design and communication skills and my active participation in action sports. Most of the ideas I've been working on for new faces are inspired by this lifestyle: fonts that are bold and fashionable and that can run down the length of a bicycle frame or the rail of a surfboard, die-cut out of vinyl, embroidered or etched; fonts that are inspired

by tattoos or scarification and that can be easily replicated; fonts that translate well on screens and can be easily animated whilst still maintaining legibility. Although my ideas for new fonts come from many sources, I believe the idea has to fulfil at least one of my four criteria in order for it to be worth designing up into a fully functional font: it should be time-less, conceptual, functional or textural. I'm sure a time will come when I have spare time to release some new faces, but until then I'll keep on riding my dirt bike and surfing my brains out in between working my butt off. I figure that if a good font is great then it won't matter if it's released now or in ten years. In the meantime I'll keep laying down new ideas and use these years to filter out the bad ideas and enjoy the great fonts that are currently out there.

Lopetz — Büro Destruct

Büro Destruct has been at the forefront of modern Swiss graphic design since the mid nineties. Their work has influenced designers all over the globe, thanks to two books about them, published by Die Gestalten Verlag. From their earliest days, they have created typefaces to fit their original style, and they decided to share a substantial part of these with other designers, for free.

When you started to create the first Büro Destruct fonts to use in your own work, you immediately released them to the public as well, and you continue to do so today...
L: Type design has always played an important part in our work. The main reason for creating original custom typefaces is to speak a unique language in our daily graphic design. The second reason is to make the resulting fonts

typedifferent.com

Opening page of Typedifferent.com, showing all Büro Destruct fonts. © 2008 Büro Destruct | Typedifferent.com

27

public and, in this way, share our type designs with other designers.

How do you decide which typefaces you will release as free fonts and which will be commercial fonts?

L: It depends on the amount of work involved with the creation of a typeface. Mostly, free fonts are fonts that don't take too much time to create. The more 'professional' we make a font (kerning work, various styles, readability), the higher the chance that it becomes a pay-font. There is always a measure of how useful a font is in the end. If we feel the font could be used for a commercial/advert for a big company with a huge budget — we're in the pay-font range.

You are a renowned graphic design studio. Do you feel this helps your free fonts to be taken more seriously by other designers?

L: Certainly our status helps the free fonts and also the pay-fonts. But we look at it the other way: our fonts helped us to become a 'renowned graphic design studio'. Compared with other font designers, our fonts may be judged less seriously, but that's in the nature of how we work on them. We treat it more like an experimental playground than very serious, hard and precise work. Our aim is not to create another Helvetica, Garamond or whatever — that would eat up years to complete. We want to create new graphic shapes that can be collected into an alphabet and make them available. That's still the same as how we started to create fonts in the early years of Büro Destruct back in 1995. The flossy font, for example, was our first

font work — it was just a collection of several poses of a sheep character.

Can you tell me what process you go through when you design your fonts? Do you first have an idea for a font or do you have an idea for a design project for which you feel the need to create a new typeface?

L: Usually, a new Büro Destruct font comes alive after the creation of a logotype, a title on a concert poster/party flyer or cd jacket. The best example is the font BD Balduin, which was initially the logo for the music artist Balduin. Sometimes a font is generated by a simple shape that we like to explore in a whole alphabet. A great source of inspiration is travelling to other countries with other languages/non-Latin alphabets like Japanese characters, Arabic characters, etc. We don't read these — we just look at shapes and reuse them in our alphabets.

Do you often reuse your existing fonts for your design work?

L: Our policy is to include them whenever it makes sense, since they speak our original language, but more often we end up using other fonts. An important reason for this is that we create fonts that are always associated with a certain project or source. They belong to that project/period. The new fonts we make are shared with other designers and it's more surprising for us to see how other designers put our fonts into their own contexts.

Top: wallpaper design to promote the BD Billding font.
Above: Full Cycle Night poster design, using BD Alm font.
Right: T-shirt design promoting the BD Wakarimasu font.
all images © 2008 Büro Destruct | Typedifferent.com

Shamrock

Shamrock (a.k.a. Jeroen Klaver) is mostly known for his gorgeous illustrations, which have a retro feel. Fewer people know that he actually holds a degree in graphic design and has created both free and pay-fonts. Many of his typefaces echo the atmosphere of his drawing style, because he creates most of them to work with his own illustrations. You really end up with part of his artistic spirit in your design when you use his fonts – they are fun, animated and irresistible.

I knew your illustrations, but not really your fonts. What place do your typefaces take in your work?
S: An important place. I started out as a graphic designer because I always loved making things like zines and flyers. I'm not the kind of designer who orders an image, puts a bit of text on top of it and sends it off. I like the things I make to be a whole. Everything needs to be well made and must be in balance. I'm also sensitive to the text; I did refuse some jobs because the writing did not make any sense. When you make everything yourself, you can do what you want! Also, I'm always interested in how things are made. I know there are always people who can do things much better then I do; but trying

things out for myself makes me really respect those people and makes it easier to communicate with them.
I started drawing letters seriously in high school. I spend a lot of time doing it and I wish I could do it more, but it just won't pay the bills. So financially my typefaces have no place at all in my work, but they are a big part of who I think I am.

Except for the Elvis typefaces, all your fonts are free fonts. Is there any specific reason for this?
S: Not all fonts are free. I have more 'commercial fonts' that are nearly finished, but I never seem to have the time to finish them and launch them properly. For years I've been saying: 'next summer (or winter, when it's summer) I'll take a few months off to get my business in order'. But I never get around to it. A lot of the free fonts are just lousy experiments, which I could not sell with a straight face – there are even a few traced old specimens among them. They were all fonts I made

Oposite, top left: design for Boomerang Freecard for 'World Animal Day', using the Shampost font and a custom type (not included in this book). Bottom left: poster for a party, using the Harum Scarum font from the Elvis font collection (not included in this book).
Far right: 4 illustrations for a cultural youth magazine, using the ShamBlock font.
all images © 2008 Shamrock int.

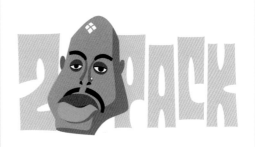

for a design job, and afterwards I decided to put them on my site. My heart is only in a few of them, and I wish I had the time to turn them into something good! I am not a supporter of free fonts per se. In fact, I think the world is clogging up with ugly designs, made by people who can't design and who think that handling a computer is all there is to it. The only thing they do is grab free things off the web and paste them together. I don't mind them doing it – I'm happy that they enjoy themselves – but the bad thing is that a lot of clients start to believe this is the way that graphic design works. On the other hand, giving away presents attracts visitors, so it might give you respect or new clients. It can also get you in touch with colleagues or musicians who use a font for a cd and then send you a copy. All nice!

Do you also design fonts without having an application in mind, or are they only made for your own needs as a designer/illustrator?
S: Yes I do, but I don't give those fonts away for free. Making fonts is a lot of work, and using specific fonts can give a designer a bit of exclusivity. I would rather see my fonts used in a nice way than abused, but I'm too busy to start selling my type in a good way. It's better that making fonts stays something I love, rather than turning into a profession that gives me headaches. Sometimes, when I'm designing something like a brochure or a little booklet or whatever, it seems easier to create a little font (or scan in some old specimens and turn them into a font) instead of going through all my fonts trying to find the right one. A lot of these I give away as free fonts.

Do you create your fonts from the point of view of a graphic designer or that of an illustrator?
S: My 'commercial type' is more personal, like my illustration work. I try to make the curves, the feel, the movement as pleasing to me as I do in my illustration and animation work. It is something I am not asked to do, unlike with design work, in which you're making something to fit the client's needs. This does not mean the designer is making something the client asks for; in this position I sometimes have to advise against my client's wishes. I think when art is at one end of the spectrum, and design at the other, illustration is exactly in the middle. It's full of personal decisions, yet it is supposed to tell the customer's story. On the other hand, designing type has a big influence on my illustration work. I work too clean. All my curves are much tighter then necessary. In an illustration that's not so bad, but in animation it costs me so much time. But I just can't resist correcting a curve in a drawing, even if it's only visible for 1/25th of a second!

Astigmatic One Eye Typographic Institute

www.astigmatic.com
astigma@astigmatic.com

Alpha Mack | Brian J. Bonislawsky

The quick brown fox jumps

ABCDEFGHIJKLMNOPQRSTUVW
xyzabcdefghijklmnopqrstuvwxyzäçéñ
0123456789(!?$¢£¥@)

Big Ruckus | Brian J. Bonislawsky

THE QUICK BROWN

ABCDEFGHIJKLMNOPQRSTUVWXYZabcd
efghijklmnopqrstuvwxyz0123456789

Buzz Saw | Brian J. Bonislawsky

THE QUICK BROWN FOX

ABCDEFGHIJKLMNOPQRSTUVWX
YZABCDEFGHIJKLMNOPQRSTUVW
XYZÄÇÉÑØÜ0123456789(&!?€)

Buzz Saw – Chipped | Brian J. Bonislawsky

THE QUICK BROWN FOX

ABCDEFGHIJKLMNOPQRSTUVWX
YZABCDEFGHIJKLMNOPQRSTUVW
XYZÄÇÉÑØÜ0123456789(&!?€)

Chicken Scratch | Brian J. Bonislawsky

QUICK BROWN

ABCDEFGHIJKLMNOPQRST
UVWXYZabcdefghijklmnopqrst
uvwxyzäçé0123456789&!?€

Ghoulish Fright | Brian J. Bonislawsky

THE QUICK BROWN

ABCDEFGHIJKLMNOPQRSTUVWXY
ZABCDEFGHIJKLMNOPQRSTUVWXY
ZÇÉÑØÜŒ0123456789(&!?$£¥€)

37

The quick brown
fox jumps
OVER
a lazy dog
Zwei Boxkämpfer
jagen Eva

Haunt — Brian J. Bonislawsky

THE QUICK BROWN

ABCDEFGHIJKLMNOPQRSTUVWXYZabcde
fghijklmnopqrstuvwxyz0123456789

Lovesick — Brian J. Bonislawsky

The quick brown fox jumps over

ABCDEFGHIJKLMNOPQRSTUVWXYZabcdefgh
ijklmnopqrstuvwxyzäçé0123456789(&:;!?$£¥€)

Nightmare — Brian J. Bonislawsky

THE QUICK BROWN FOX

ABCDEFGHIJKLMNOPQRSTUVW
XYZABCDEFGHIJKLMNOPQRSTUV
WXYZÄÇÉÑ0123456789(!?$£¥€)

Papa Mano | Brian J. Bonislawsky

QUICK BROWN

ABCDEFGHIJKLMNOPQRST
UVWXYZABCDEFGHIJKLMNOPQRS
TUVWXYZ0123456789(&!?$£¥€)

Tibetian Beefgarden | Brian J. Bonislawsky

THE QUICK BROWN

ABCDEFGHIJKLMNOPQRSTUV
wXYZabcdefghijklmnopqrstuvw
xyzäéñöü0123456789(&.,.!?$¢£¥€)

Wild Monkeys | Brian J. Bonislawsky

THE QUICK BROWN FOX

ABCDEFGHIJKLMNOPQRSTUVwXYZABC
DEFGHIJKLMNOPQRSTUVwXYZ0123456789!?

Dreiecke	Boris Schandert

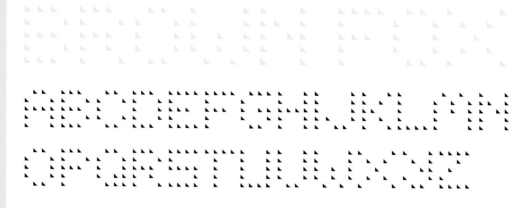

My – Regular	Boris Schandert

THE QUICK BROWN

ABCDEFGHIJKLMNOPQRSTUV
WXYZÄÖÜ012345678(&!?)

THE QUICK BROWN FOX JUMPS OVER A LAZY DOG. ZWEI BOXKÄMPFER JAGEN EVA QUER
DURCH SYLT. LOREM IPSUM DOLOR SIT AMET, CONSECTETUR ADIPISICING ELIT, SED DO
EIUSMOD TEMPOR INCIDIDUNT UT LABORE ET DOLORE MAGNA ALIQUA. THE QUICK BROWN

My – Bold	Boris Schandert

THE QUICK BROWN

ABCDEFGHIJKLMNOPQRSTUV
WXYZÄÖÜ012345678(&!?)

THE QUICK BROWN FOX JUMPS OVER A LAZY DOG. ZWEI BOXKÄMPFER JAGEN EVA QUER
DURCH SYLT. LOREM IPSUM DOLOR SIT AMET, CONSECTETUR ADIPISICING ELIT, SED DO
EIUSMOD TEMPOR INCIDIDUNT UT LABORE ET DOLORE MAGNA ALIQUA. THE QUICK BROWN

THE QUICK
BROWN
FOX JUMPS OVER
A LAZY DOG
LOREM
IPSUM DOLOR

| Slimbo | Boris Schandert |

QUICK BROWN FOX

Regular

ABCDEFGHIJKLMNOPQR
STUVWXYZ0123456789

Medium

ABCDEFGHIJKLMNOPQR
STUVWXYZ0123456789

Bold

ABCDEFGHIJKLMNOPQR
STUVWXYZ0123456789

| Subtract | Boris Schandert |

QUICK BROWN

ABCDEFGHIJKLM
NOPQRSTUVWXYZ
0123456789.,::!?

Brain Eaters Font Co.

www.braineaters.com
info@braineaters.com

Action Is | Brad Nelson

JUMPS OVER

ABCDEFGHIJKLMNOPQRST
UVWXYZ0123456789&!?

Decaying Kuntry | Brad Nelson

The quick brown

ABCDEFGHIJKLMNOPQRSTU
VWXYZabcdefghijklmnopqr
stuvwxyz0123456789(&!?$@)

Marker Monkey | Brad Nelson

The QUICK BROWN FOX

ABCDEFGHiJKLMNOPQRSTUVWXY
ZaBcdefghijKLMNOPQRSTUVWXYZ
0123456789(&:;!?$¢£©)

Maverick | Brad Nelson

QUICK BROWN
FOX JUMPS

ABCDEFGHIJKLMNOPQR
STUVWXYZ0123456789?

Musicals | Brad Nelson

QUICK BROWN

ABCDEFGHIJKLMNOPQRS
TUVWXYZ0123456789!?

Stencil Gothic | Brad Nelson

FOX JUMPS OVER

ABCDEFGHIJKLMNOPQRST
UVWXYZabcdefghijklmnopqr
stuvwxyz0123456789(&!?)

Tattoo Girl | Brad Nelson

The quick brown

ABCDEFGHIJKLMNOPQR
STUVWXYZabcdefghijKlm
nopqrstuvwxyz0123456789&

Thats Super | Brad Nelson

BROWN FOX

ABCDEFGHIJKL
MNOPQRSTUVW
XYZ0123456789

Witless | Brad Nelson

BROWN FOX
JUMPS OVER A LAZY

ABCDEFGHiJKLMNOPQRS
TUVWXYZ0123456789&!?

Brode Vosloo

brode@bolditalic.co.za

ErrorType8 | Brode Vosloo

BROWN FOX

A B C D E F G H i j k L M N O P Q R
S t U V W X Y Z 0 1 2 3 4 5 6 7 8 9

Holier | Brode Vosloo

BROWN FOX

A B © D E F G H I J K L M N O P Q R S T U
V W X Y Z @ 6 ¢ d e f g h i j k l m n o p q
® s t u v w x y z 0 1 2 3 4 5 6 7 8 9 (&!?)

I Alfabhethi | Brode Vosloo

THE QUICK BROWN

A B C D E F G H I J K L M N O P Q R S T
U V W X Y Z a b c d e f g h i j K L m n o p q
r s t u v w x y z 0 1 2 3 4 5 6 7 8 9 (&·,;!?)

Quick brown

ABCDEFGHIJKLMNOPQRST
UVWXYZabcdefghijklmnop
qrstuvwxyz0123456789&!?

Quick brown

ABCDEFGHIJKLMNOPQRST
UVWXYZabcdefghijklmnop
qrstuvwxyz0123456789&!?

THE QUICK BROWN

ABCDEFGHIJKLMNOPQRSTUV
WXYZabcdefghijklMNopqrstuv
wxyz0123456789 :;!?◄►

Brode Vosloo

THE QUICK
BROWN
FOX JUMPS
OVER A LAZY DOG
LOREM
IPSUM DOLOR
SIT AMET
CONSECTETUR

Pleine Str | Brode Vosloo

The quick brown

ABCDEFghijKLMnopqrst
uvwxyzaBCDEfghijKLmn
opqrstuvwxyz&.;;

Rural | Brode Vosloo

FOX JUMPS
OVER a LAZY DOG

aBCDEFGhijKLMNOPQRS
TUVWXYZ0123456789:;:

Scripteria Toid | Brode Vosloo

The quick brown fox

ABCDEFGHIJKLMNOPQ
RSTUVWXYZabcdefghijklm
nopqrstuvwxyzäçéîñ0123456789!?

QUICK BROWN

ABCDEFGHIJKLMNOPQRSTU
VWXYZabcDefghijklmnopqrs
tuvwxyz0123456789(&:;!?)

Bumbayo Font Fabrik

www.bumbayo.extra.hu
bumbayo@gmail.com

3rd Man | Attila Zigó

THE QUICK BROWN

ABCDEFGHIJKLMNOPQRSTUVWXYZABCDE
FGHIJKLMNOPQRSTUVWXYZ0123456789

Baron Kuffner | Attila Zigó

BROWN FOX

ABCDEFGHIJKLMNOPQRSTUVWXYZABCDEF
GHIJKLMNOPQRSTUVWXYZ0123456789&!?

Conrad Veidt | Attila Zigó

BROWN FOX

ABCDEFGHIJKLMNOPQRSTUVWXYZabc
defghijklmnopqrstuvwxyz0123456789&

Deutschische | Attila Zigó

The quick brown fox jumps

ABCDEFGHIJKLMNOPQ
RSTUVWXYZabcdefghijklmnop
qrstuvwxyz0123456789(:;!?$@)

Fibyngerowa | Attila Zigó

THE QUICK BROWN

ABCDEFGHIJKLMNOPQRSTUVWXYZabcde
fghijklmnopqrstuvwxyz0123456789&

Gipsiero | Attila Zigó

BROWN FOX

ABCDEFGHIJKLM
NOPQRSTUVWXY
Z0123456789(&$@)

Kyselak — Attila Zigó

THE QUICK BROWN FOX

THE QUICK BROWN FOX JUMPS OVER A LAZY

ABCDEFGHIJKLMNOPQRSTUVWXYZ0123456789&!?

Matejino — Attila Zigó

THE QUICK BROWN

FOX JUMPS OVER A LAZY DOG

ABCDEFGHIJKLMNOPQRSTUVWXYZ0123456789

Pokoljaro — Attila Zigó

The quick brown

ABCDEFGHIJKLMNOPQR
STUVWXYZabcdefghijklmno
opqrstuvwxyz012345678(&!?)

8-bit — Derek Clark

quick brown

abcdefghijklmnopqrs
tuvwxyz0123456789

Commando — Derek Clark

BROWN FOX

ABCDEFGHIJKLMNOPQR
STUVWXYZ0123456789

Defaulterror — Derek Clark

the quick brown

abcdefghijklmnopqrs
tuvwxyz0123456789

the quick brown fox jumpS over a lazy dog lorem

Dirty Flamingo | Derek Clark

brown fox
jumps over a lazy

abcdefghijklmnopqrstuvwxyz

el Diablo | Derek Clark

brown fox jumps over

abcdefghijklmnopqrstuvwxyz

Pooplatter | Derek Clark

brown fox
jumps over a lazy dog

abcdefghi jklmnopqrStuvwxyz

Dieter Steffmann

www.steffmann.de
dieter@steffmann.de

Chelsea — Dieter Steffmann

ABCDEFGHIJKLMNOPQRSTU
VWXYZabcdefghijklmnopqrst
uvwxyzäçéñø0123456789(&:;!?)

THE QUICK BROWN FOX jumps over a lazy dog. Zwei Boxkämpfer jagen Eva quer durch Sylt. Lorem ipsum dolor sit amet, consectetur adipisicing elit, sed do eiusmod tempor incididunt ut labore et dolore magna aliqua. The quick brown fox jumps over

Chopin Script — Dieter Steffmann

The quick brown fox

ABCDEFGHIJKLMNO
PQRSTUVWXYZabcdefghijklmn
opqrstuvwxyzäçéíñü0123456789(&:;!?$)

Fette deutsche Schrift — Dieter Steffmann

ABCDEFGHIJKLMNOPQRSTU
VWXYZabcdefghijklmnopqrstuvwxy
zäçéîñøú0123456789(&.,:;!?$¢£¥€)

THE QUICK BROWN FOX jumps over a lazy dog. Zwei Boxkämpfer jagen Eva quer durch Sylt. Lorem ipsum dolor sit amet, consectetur adipisicing elit, sed do eiusmod tempor incididunt ut labore et dolore magna aliqua. The quick brown fox jumps over a lazy

Fette Trump-Deutsch | Dieter Steffmann

Quick brown fox

ABCDEFGHIJKLMNOPQ
RSTUVWXYZabcdefghijklm
nopqrstuvwxyz0123456789&!?

Forelle | Dieter Steffmann

The quick brown fox jumps

ABCDEFGHIJKLMNOPQ
RSTUVWXYZabcdefghijklmno
pqrstuvwxyzäçéñ0123456789(&:;!?$£¥)

Frederick Text | Dieter Steffmann

ABCDEFGHIJKLMNOPQR
STUVWXYZabcdefghijklmnopqrs
tuvwxyzäçéñø0123456789(&.,:;!?$£¥)

THE QUICK BROWN FOX jumps over a lazy dog. Zwei Boxkämpfer jagen Eva
quer durch Sylt. Lorem ipsum dolor sit amet, consectetur adipisicing elit, sed do eiusmod
tempor incididunt ut labore et dolore magna aliqua. The quick brown fox jumps over a lazy

65

Dieter Steffmann

Ganz Grobe Gotisch | Dieter Steffmann

ABCDEFGHIJKLMNOP
QRSTUVWXYZabcdefghijk
lmnopqrstuvwxy0123456789!?

Goudy Mediaeval | Dieter Steffmann

ABCDEFGHIJKLMNOPQRST
UVWXYZabcdefghijklmnopqrstuvwx
yzăçéîñøŭœ0123456789(&.,:;!?$£¥)

The QUICK BROWN FOX jumps over a lazy dog. Zwei Boxkämpfer jagen Eva quer durch Sylt. Lorem ipsum dolor sit amet, consectetur adipisicing elit, sed do eiusmod tempor incididunt ut labore et dolore magna aliqua. The quick brown fox jumps over a lazy dog. Zwei

Goudy Thirty | Dieter Steffmann

ABCDEFGHIJKLMNOPQRSTUV
WXYZabcdefghijklmnopqrstuvwx
yzäçéîñøüo123456789(&.,:;!?$£¥)

THE QUICK BROWN FOX jumps over a lazy dog. Zwei Boxkämpfer jagen Eva quer durch Sylt. Lorem ipsum dolor sit amet, consectetur adipisicing elit, sed do eiusmod tempor incididunt ut labore et dolore magna aliqua. The quick brown fox

QUICK BROWN

ABCDEFGHIJKLMNO
PQRSTUVWXYZÄÉÎÑ
ØÜŒ0123456789(&.,;:!?$)

The quick brown fox jumps

ABCDEFGHIJKLMNOPQRST
UVWXYZabcdefghijklmnopqrstuvwx
yzäçéîñøšüœ0123456789(&:;!?$€¥)

ABCDEFGHIJKLMNOPQR
STUVWXYZabcdefghijklmnopqrst
uvwxyzäçéîñøšüœ0123456789(&:;!?$)

THE QUICK BROWN FOX jumps over a lazy dog. Zwei Boxkämpfer jagen Eva
quer durch Sylt. Lorem ipsum dolor sit amet, consectetur adipisicing elit, sed do eiusmod
tempor incididunt ut labore et dolore magna aliqua. The quick brown fox jumps over a lazy

Quick brown

ABCDEFGHIJKLMNOPQRS
TUVWXYZabcdefghijklmno
pqrstuvwxyz0123456789&!?

The quick brown fox

ABCDEFGHIJKLMNOPQRS
TUVWXYZabcdefghijklmnopq
rstuvwxyzäçéñ0123456789(&!?)

ABCDEFGHIJKLMNOPQRS
TUVWXYZabcdefghijklmnopqrs
tuvwxyzäçéñø0123456789(&!?)

THE QUICK BROWN FOX jumps over a lazy dog. Zwei Boxkämpfer jagen
Eva quer durch Sylt. Lorem ipsum dolor sit amet, consectetur adipisicing elit, sed
do eiusmod tempor incididunt ut labore et dolore magna aliqua. The quick brown

The quick brown fox jumps over a LAZY DOG

Zwei Boxkämpfer jagen Eva

Maximilian Zier | Dieter Steffmann

Brown fox jumps

ABCDE FGHIJKLM
NOPQRSTUVWXYZ

Mayflower Antique | Dieter Steffmann

ABCDEFGHIJKLMNOPQ
RSTUVWXYZabcdefghijklmn
opqrstuvwxyz0123456789

THE QUICK BROWN FOX jumps over a lazy dog. Zwei Boxkämpfer
jagen Eva quer durch Sylt. Lorem ipsum dolor sit amet, consectetur adipisicing elit, sed do eiusmod tempor incididunt ut labore et dolore magna

Pinewood | Dieter Steffmann

JUMPS OVER A LAZY

ABCDEFGHIJKLMNOPQR
QRSTUVWXYZÁÇÉÍNÖÜ
0123456789(&.,;:!?$)

Powell Antique — Dieter Steffmann

ABCDEFGHIJKLMNOPQ
RSTUVWXYZabcdefghijklm
nopqrstuvwxyz0123456789(&!?)

THE QUICK BROWN FOX jumps over a lazy dog. Zwei Boxkämpfer jagen Eva quer durch Sylt. Lorem ipsum dolor sit amet, consectetur adipisicing elit, sed do eiusmod tempor incididunt ut labore et dolore magna aliqua. The

Reeperbahn — Dieter Steffmann

Quick brown fox jumps over a

ABCDEFGHIJKLMNOPQRST
UVWXYZabcdefghijklmnopqrstuv
wxyzäöü0123456789(&.,:!?$)

Schmale Anzeigenschrift — Dieter Steffmann

Quick brown fox jumps

ABCDEFGHIJKLMNOPQRSTU
VWXYZabcdefghijklmnopqrstuvwx
yzäçéîñöüœ0123456789(&.,:;!?$£¥€)

Schmale Anzeigenschrift Zier | Dieter Steffmann

The Quick Brown Fox

ABCDEFGHIJKLM
NOPQRSTUVWXYZ

Theuerdank Fraktur | Dieter Steffmann

Quick brown fox jumps

ABCDEFGHIJKLMNOPQR
STUVWXYZabcdefghijklmnopqr
stuvwxyzäçñø0123456789(&:;!?$!?)

Tribeca | Dieter Steffmann

QUICK BROWN

ABCDEFGHIJKLMNOPQ
RSTUVWXYZÄÇÉÑÖØÜ
0123456789(&.,:;!?)

The quick brown

ABCDEFGHIJKLMNOPQRSTU
VWXYZabcdefghijklmnopqrst
uvwxyzăçéñø0123456789(&:;!?$)

The quick brown fox

ABCDEFGHIJKLMNOPQRSTUVWX
YZabcdefghijklmnopqrstuvwxyzăçéñ
0123456789(&.,:;!?$£¥€)

The quick brown fox

ABCDEFGHIJKLMNOPQ
RSTUVWXYZabcdefghijklmno
pqrstuvwxyzăéñø0123456789(&!?)

ABCDEFGHIJKLMNOPQRSTU
VWXYZabcdefghijklmnopqrst
uvwxyzäçéñø0123456789(&!?)

THE QUICK BROWN FOX jumps over a lazy dog. Zwei Boxkämpfer jagen Eva quer durch Sylt. Lorem ipsum dolor sit amet, consectetur adipisicing elit, sed do eiusmod tempor incididunt ut labore et dolore magna aliqua. The quick brown fox

ABCDEFGHIJKLMNOPQRST
UVWXYZabcdefghijklmnopq
rstuvwxyzäçñ0123456789(&!?)

THE QUICK BROWN FOX jumps over a lazy dog. Zwei Boxkämpfer jagen Eva quer durch Sylt. Lorem ipsum dolor sit amet, consectetur adipisicing elit, sed do eiusmod tempor incididunt ut labore et dolore magna aliqua. The quick brown fox

The quick brown

ABCDEFGHIJKLMNOPQRST
UVWXYZabcdefghijklmnopqrst
uvwxyzäçéñő0123456789(&:;!?$£)

eightface

www.eightface.com
dave@eightface.com

| Adlock | Dave Kellam |

THE QUICK BROWN FOX
JUMPS OVER

ABCDEFGHIJKLMNOPQRST
UVWXYZ0123456789(:;!?@)

| After Shok | Dave Kellam |

QUICK BROWN
FOX JUMPS

ABCDEFGHIJKLMNOPQR
STUVWXYZ0123456789

| Cof | Dave Kellam |

A LAZY DOG

ABCDEFGHIJKLMNOPQRS
TUVWXYZabcdefghijklmnop
qrstuvwxyz0123456789¢!?

Dawg Box | Dave Kellam

BROWN FOX

ABCDEFGHIJKLMNOPQRS
TUVWXYZ0123456789c

Discount Inferno | Dave Kellam

THE QUICK BROWN

ABCDEFGHIJKLMNOPQRST
UVWXYZabcdefghijklmnopq
rstuvwxyz0123456789&!?

Eau de Toilet | Dave Kellam

THE QUICK BROWN
FOX JUMPS

ABCDEFGHIJKLMNOPQRS
TUVWXYZ0123456789

THE QUICK BROWN FOX JUMPS OVER A LAZY DOG LOREM IPSUM DOLOR SIT AMET CONSECTETUR

Grade	Dave Kellam

BROWN FOX

ABCDEFGHIJKLMNOPQRS
TUVWXYZabcdefghij klmno
pqrstuvwxyz0123456789(!?)

Issac	Dave Kellam

Quick brown

ABCDEFGHIJKLMN
OPQRSTUVWXYZabcde
fghijklmnopqrstuvwxyz0123456789&

MillionAir	Dave Kellam

The quick brown

ABCDEFGHIJKLMNOPQRSTU
VWXYZabcdefghijklmnopqr
stuvwxyz0123456789(&:;!?)

THE QUICK BROWN FOX
JUMPS OVER

ABCDEFGHIJKLMNOPQR
STUVWXYZ0123456789?

THE QUICK BROWN FOX
JUMPS OVER

ABCDEFGHIJKLMNOPQR
STUVWXYZ0123456789?

THE QUICK BROWN
FOX JUMPS OVER

ABCDEFGHIJKLMNO
PQRSTUVWXYZA

exljbris

www.exljbris.nl
jos@exljbris.nl

Anivers – Regular   Jos Buivenga

ABCDEFGHIJKLMNOPQRSTUV
WXYZabcdefghijklmnopqrstuv
wxyząčéǵo123456789(&:;!?$€)

THE QUICK BROWN FOX jumps over a lazy dog. Zwei Boxkämpfer jagen Eva quer durch Sylt. Lorem ipsum dolor sit amet, consectetur adipisicing elit, sed do eiusmod tempor incididunt ut labore et dolore magna aliqua. The quick brown fox jumps over a lazy dog. Zwei Boxkämp-

Delicious – Roman   Jos Buivenga

ABCDEFGHIJKLMNOPQRSTUVW
XYZabcdefghijklmnopqrstuvw
xyzäçéñøo123456789(&:;!?$€)

THE QUICK BROWN FOX jumps over a lazy dog. Zwei Boxkämpfer jagen Eva quer durch Sylt. Lorem ipsum dolor sit amet, consectetur adipisicing elit, sed do eiusmod tempor incididunt ut labore et dolore magna aliqua. The quick brown fox jumps over a lazy dog. Zwei Boxkämpfer

Delicious – Italic   Jos Buivenga

ABCDEFGHIJKLMNOPQRSTUVW
XYZabcdefghijklmnopqrstuvw
xyzäçéñøo123456789(&:;!?€)

THE QUICK BROWN FOX jumps over a lazy dog. Zwei Boxkämpfer jagen Eva quer durch Sylt. Lorem ipsum dolor sit amet, consectetur adipisicing elit, sed do eiusmod tempor incididunt ut labore et dolore magna aliqua. The quick brown fox jumps over a lazy dog. Zwei Boxkämpfer

ABCDEFGHIJKLMNOPQRSTUVW
XYZABCDEFGHIJKLMNOPQRSTUV
WXYZÄÇÉÑØ0123456789(&!?€)

THE QUICK BROWN FOX JUMPS OVER A LAZY DOG. ZWEI BOXKÄMPFER JAGEN EVA QUER DURCH SYLT.
LOREM IPSUM DOLOR SIT AMET, CONSECTETUR ADIPISICING ELIT, SED DO EIUSMOD TEMPOR INCIDI-
DUNT UT LABORE ET DOLORE MAGNA ALIQUA. THE QUICK BROWN FOX JUMPS OVER A LAZY DOG. ZWEI

ABCDEFGHIJKLMNOPQRSTUVW
XYZabcdefghijklmnopqrstuvw
xyzäçéñø0123456789(&:;!?$€)

THE QUICK BROWN FOX jumps over a lazy dog. Zwei Boxkämpfer jagen Eva quer durch Sylt.
Lorem ipsum dolor sit amet, consectetur adipisicing elit, sed do eiusmod tempor incididunt ut
labore et dolore magna aliqua. The quick brown fox jumps over a lazy dog. Zwei Boxkämpfer

ABCDEFGHIJKLMNOPQRSTUVW
XYZabcdefghijklmnopqrstuvw
xyzäçéñø0123456789(℮:;!?€)

THE QUICK BROWN FOX jumps over a lazy dog. Zwei Boxkämpfer jagen Eva quer durch Sylt.
Lorem ipsum dolor sit amet, consectetur adipisicing elit, sed do eiusmod tempor incididunt ut
labore et dolore magna aliqua. The quick brown fox jumps over a lazy dog. Zwei Boxkämpfer

ABCDEFGHIJKLMNOPQRSTUVW XYZabcdefghijklmnopqrstuv wxyzäçéñø0123456789(&!?€)

THE QUICK BROWN FOX jumps over a lazy dog. Zwei Boxkämpfer jagen Eva quer durch Sylt. Lorem ipsum dolor sit amet, consectetur adipisicing elit, sed do eiusmod tempor incididunt ut labore et dolore magna aliqua. The quick brown fox jumps over a lazy dog. Zwei Boxkämpfer

ABCDEFGHIJKLMNOPQRSTUV WXYZabcdefghijklmnopqrstuvw xyząčégñ0123456789(&:;!?$€)

THE QUICK BROWN FOX jumps over a lazy dog. Zwei Boxkämpfer jagen Eva quer durch Sylt. Lorem ipsum dolor sit amet, consectetur adipisicing elit, sed do eiusmod tempor incididunt ut labore et dolore magna aliqua. The quick brown fox jumps over a lazy dog.

ABCDEFGHIJKLMNOPQRSTUV WXYZabcdefghijklmnopqrstuv wxyząčégñ0123456789(&!?€)

THE QUICK BROWN FOX jumps over a lazy dog. Zwei Boxkämpfer jagen Eva quer durch Sylt. Lorem ipsum dolor sit amet, consectetur adipisicing elit, sed do eiusmod tempor incididunt ut labore et dolore magna aliqua. The quick brown fox jumps over a lazy dog.

exljbris | www.exljbris.nl

The quick brown fox jumps over A LAZY DOG Zwei Boxkämpfer jagen Eva

ABCDEFGHIJKLMNOPQRSTU VWXYZabcdefghijklmnopqrs tuvwxyząéġ0123456789&!?€

THE QUICK BROWN FOX jumps over a lazy dog. Zwei Boxkämpfer jagen Eva quer durch Sylt. Lorem ipsum dolor sit amet, consectetur adipisicing elit, sed do eiusmod tempor incididunt ut labore et dolore magna aliqua. The quick brown fox jumps over

ABCDEFGHIJKLMNOPQRSTU VWXYZabcdefghijklmnopqrs tuvwxyząéč0123456789!?€

THE QUICK BROWN FOX jumps over a lazy dog. Zwei Boxkämpfer jagen Eva quer durch Sylt. Lorem ipsum dolor sit amet, consectetur adipisicing elit, sed do eius-mod tempor incididunt ut labore et dolore magna aliqua. The quick brown fox

ABCDEFGHIJKLMNOPQRST UVWXYZabcdefghijklmnop qrstuvwxyz0123456789!?

THE QUICK BROWN FOX jumps over a lazy dog. Zwei Boxkämpfer jagen Eva quer durch Sylt. Lorem ipsum dolor sit amet, consectetur adipisicing elit, sed do eiusmod tempor incididunt ut labore et dolore magna aliqua. The quick

ABCDEFGHIJKLMNOPQRST UVWXYZabcdefghijklmnop qrstuvwxyz0123456789&!?€

THE QUICK BROWN FOX jumps over a lazy dog. Zwei Boxkämpfer jagen Eva quer durch Sylt. Lorem ipsum dolor sit amet, consectetur adipisicing elit, sed do eiusmod tempor incididunt ut labore et dolore magna aliqua. The quick brown fox jumps

ABCDEFGHIJKLMNOPQRSTUV WXYZabcdefghijklmnopqrstu vwxyzäçéñø0123456789&:;!?€

THE QUICK BROWN FOX jumps over a lazy dog. Zwei Boxkämpfer jagen Eva quer durch Sylt. Lorem ipsum dolor sit amet, consectetur adipisicing elit, sed do eiusmod tempor incididunt ut labore et dolore magna aliqua. The quick brown fox jumps over

ABCDEFGHIJKLMNOPQRSTUV WXYZabcdefghijklmnopqrstuv wxyzäçéñø0123456789(&:;!?$€)

THE QUICK BROWN FOX jumps over a lazy dog. Zwei Boxkämpfer jagen Eva quer durch Sylt. Lorem ipsum dolor sit amet, consectetur adipisicing elit, sed do eiusmod tempor incididunt ut labore et dolore magna aliqua. The quick brown fox jumps over a lazy dog.

ABCDEFGHIJKLMNOPQRSTU VWXYZABCDEFGHIJKLMNOPQR STUVWXYZÄÇÉ0123456789&:;!?

THE QUICK BROWN FOX JUMPS OVER A LAZY DOG. ZWEI BOXKÄMPFER JAGEN EVA QUER DURCH SYLT. LOREM IPSUM DOLOR SIT AMET, CONSECTETUR ADIPISICING ELIT, SED DO EIUS-MOD TEMPOR INCIDIDUNT UT LABORE ET DOLORE MAGNA ALIQUA. THE QUICK BROWN FOX

ABCDEFGHIJKLMNOPQRSTU VWXYZabcdefghijklmnopqr stuvwxyzäçéñ0123456789&!?

THE QUICK BROWN FOX jumps over a lazy dog. Zwei Boxkämpfer jagen Eva quer durch Sylt. Lorem ipsum dolor sit amet, consectetur adipisicing elit, sed do eius-mod tempor incididunt ut labore et dolore magna aliqua. The quick brown fox

ABCDEFGHIJKLMNOPQRSTUV WXYZabcdefghijklmnopqrstu vwxyzäçéñ0123456789&:;!?$€

THE QUICK BROWN FOX jumps over a lazy dog. Zwei Boxkämpfer jagen Eva quer durch Sylt. Lorem ipsum dolor sit amet, consectetur adipisicing elit, sed do eiusmod tempor incididunt ut labore et dolore magna aliqua. The quick brown fox jumps over a lazy

ABCDEFGHIJKLMNOPQRSTUV
WXYZabcdefghijklmnopqrstuv
wxyzäçéñøœ0123456789&:;!?€

THE QUICK BROWN FOX jumps over a lazy dog. Zwei Boxkämpfer jagen Eva quer durch Sylt. Lorem ipsum dolor sit amet, consectetur adipisicing elit, sed do eiusmod tempor incididunt ut labore et dolore magna aliqua. The quick brown fox jumps over a lazy dog. Zwei

ABCDEFGHIJKLMNOPQRSTUV
WXYZABCDEFGHIJKLMNOPQRS
TUVWXYZÄÇÉ0123456789&!?€

THE QUICK BROWN FOX JUMPS OVER A LAZY DOG. ZWEI BOXKÄMPFER JAGEN EVA QUER DURCH SYLT. LOREM IPSUM DOLOR SIT AMET, CONSECTETUR ADIPISICING ELIT, SED DO EIUSMOD TEMPOR INCIDIDUNT UT LABORE ET DOLORE MAGNA ALIQUA. THE QUICK

ABCDEFGHIJKLMNOPQRSTU
VWXYZabcdefghijklmnopqrs
tuvwxyzäçé0123456789&!?€

THE QUICK BROWN FOX jumps over a lazy dog. Zwei Boxkämpfer jagen Eva quer durch Sylt. Lorem ipsum dolor sit amet, consectetur adipisicing elit, sed do eiusmod tempor incididunt ut labore et dolore magna aliqua. The quick brown fox jumps over

ABCDEFGHIJKLMNOPQRSTU VWXYZabcdefghijklmnopqrst uvwxyzäçéñø0123456789&!?€

THE QUICK BROWN FOX jumps over a lazy dog. Zwei Boxkämpfer jagen Eva quer durch Sylt. Lorem ipsum dolor sit amet, consectetur adipisicing elit, sed do eiusmod tempor incididunt ut labore et dolore magna aliqua. The quick brown fox jumps over a lazy dog.

ABCDEFGHIJKLMNOPQRSTU VWXYZabcdefghijklmnopqrstuv wxyzäçéñọ0123456789(&:;!?Ṣ€£¥)

THE QUICK BROWN FOX jumps over a lazy dog. Zwei Boxkämpfer jagen Eva quer durch Sylt. Lorem ipsum dolor sit amet, consectetur adipisicing elit, sed do eiusmod tempor incididunt ut labore et dolore magna aliqua. The quick brown fox jumps over a lazy dog. Zwei

Fenotype

www.fenotype.com
emil.bertell@fenotype.com

10.10 | Emil Bertell

The quick brown fox jumps over a lazy

abcdefghijklmnopqrstuvwxyz

79 | Emil Bertell

FOX JUMPS OVER

ABCDEFGHIJKLM
NOPQRSTUVWXYZ
0123456789&!?

Blockbusta | Emil Bertell

JUMPS OVER

ABCDEFGHIJKLMNOPQRS
TUVWXYZ0123456789!?

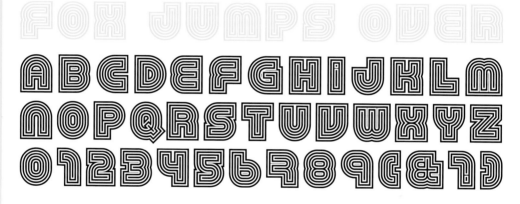

Digital Kauno | Emil Bertell

Brown fox

ABCDEFGHIJKLMNOPQRSTUVWXYZabcd.
efghijklmnopqrstuvwxyz0123456789?

Disco 1 | Emil Bertell

the quick brown

abcdefghijklmnopqrstuvwxyz0123456789

Disco 3 | Emil Bertell

brown fox

abcdefghijklmnopqrstuvwxyz0123456789

93

the quick
BROWN
fox jumph over
a lazy, dog
Lorem iphum

FUTU	Emil Bertell

quick brown
fox jumps over

abcdefghijklmn
opqrstuvwxyz

Genotype	Emil Bertell

the quick
brown fox

abcdefghijklmn
opqrstuvwxyzä

HKI metropol	Emil Bertell

fox jumps over

abcdefghijklmn
opqrstuvwxyzäö
0123456789&!?

HKI Nightlife — Emil Bertell

quick brown

a b c d e f g h i j k l m
n o p q r s t u v w x y z
0 1 2 3 4 5 6 7 8 9 & ! ?

Lastu #2 — Emil Bertell

fox jumps over

a b c d e f g h i j k l m n o
p q r s t u v w x y z . , ; : ! ?

Letters — Emil Bertell

BROWN FOX

A B C D E F G H I J K L M N O P Q R S
T U V W X Y Z 0 1 2 3 4 5 6 7 8 9 ! ?

BROWN FOX

ABCDEFGHIJKLMNOPQR
STUVWXYZ0123456789

Linja | Emil Bertell

The quick brown fox jumps over

ABCDEFGHIJKLMNOPQRSTUVWXYZabcde
fghijklmnopqrstuvwxyz0123456789&

Nippon Blocks | Emil Bertell

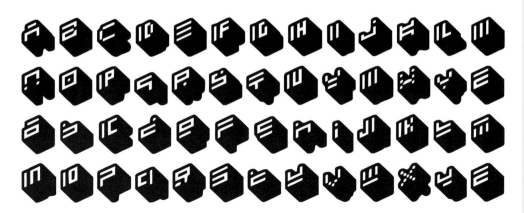

FOX JUMPS

ABCDEFGHIJKLMNOPQRSTUVWXYZabcd
efghijklmnopqrstuvwxyz0123456789

BROWN

ABCDEFGHIJKLMNOPQ
RSTUVWXYZabcdefgh
ijklmnopqrstuvwxyz

QUICK BROWN FOX
JUMPS OVER A LAZY DOG

ABCDEFGHIJKLMNOPQRST
UVWXYZ0123456789(&:;!?)

| Samarin | Emil Bertell |

THE QUICK BROWN

ABCDEFGHIJKLMN
OPQRSTUVWXYZ
Ö Ü 0 1 2 3 4 5 6 7 8 9 1 7

| Simpletype | Emil Bertell |

BROWN FOX

ABCDEFGHIJKLMNOPQRSTU
VWXYZABCDEFGHIJKLMNOP
QRSTUVWXYZ0123456789?

| TANTOR | Emil Bertell |

QUICK BROWN
FOX JUMPS OVER A

ABCDEFGHIJKLMMN
OPQRSTUVWXYYZ!

FOX JUMPS OVER

ABCDEFGHiJKLMNOPQRSTU
VWXYZabCdefGhiJKLMNOP
QrStUVWXYZ0123456789:!

quick brown

ABCDEFGHiJKLMNOPQRSTU
VWXYZabCdefGhiJKLMNOP
QrStUVWXYZ0123456789!

QUICK BROWN
FOX JUMPS OVER

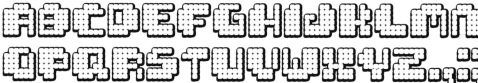

ABCDEFGHIJKLMN
OPQRSTUVWXYZ...;;

Fenotype | www.fenotype.com

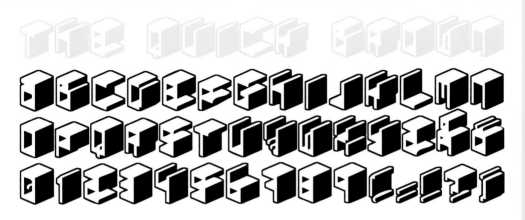

ABCD3FGHIJKLMNOP&RSTU
VWXYZabcdef9hijKLMNOP
qRSRSruvwxyz0123456789

ABCD3FGHIJKLMNOP&RSTU
VWXYZabcdef9hijKLMNOP
PqRSruvwxyz0123456789

URAL Phat | Emil Bertell

BROWN FOX

ABCD3FGHIJKLMNOPQRSTU
VWXYZAbcdefghijKLMNOP
qRSTUVWXYZ0123456789

URAL Thin | Emil Bertell

THE QUICK BROWN

ABCD3FGHIJKLMNOPQRSTU
VWXYZAbcdefghijKLMNOP
qRSTUVWXYZ0123456789

Valimo | Emil Bertell

QUICK BROWN

ABCD3FGHIJKLMNOPQRSTU
VWXYZabcdefghijKLMNOP
qRstUVWXYZ0123456789!

Flat-it type foundry

www.flat-it.com
info@flat-it.com

THE QUICK BROWN

ABCDEFGHIJKLMNOPQRST
UVWXYZ0123456789(&!?)

Blackout3 – Extra Light | Ryoichi Tsunekawa

quick brown

abcdefghijklmnopqrstuvwxyzabcde
fghijklmnopqrstuvwxyz0123456789

Blackout3 – Light | Ryoichi Tsunekawa

quick brown

abcdefghijklmnopqrstuvwxyzabcdefg
hijklmnopqrstuvwxyz0123456789&!?

104

Blackout3 – Regular | Ryoichi Tsunekawa

quick brown

abcdefghijklmnopqrstuvwxyzabcdefghi
jklmnopqrstuvwxyzåææœ0123456789â!?

Blackout3 Plus1 – Extra Light | Ryoichi Tsunekawa

brown fox jumps

abcdefghijklmnopqrstuvwxyzabcde
fghijklmnopqrstuvwxyz0123456789

Blackout3 Plus1 – Light | Ryoichi Tsunekawa

brown fox jumps

abcdefghijklmnopqrstuvwxyzabcdefg
hijklmnopqrstuvwxyzæœ0123456789!?

Blackout3 Plus1 – Regular | Ryoichi Tsunekawa

brown fox jumps

abcdefghijklmnopqrstuvwxyzabcdefghi
jklmnopqrstuvwxyzåæœ0123456789ø!?

Canstop | Ryoichi Tsunekawa

QUICK bROWN

ABCDEFGHIJKLMNOPQRSTUVW
XYZABCDEFGHIJKLMNOPQ
RSTUVWXYZ0123456789

Ego | Ryoichi Tsunekawa

THE QUICK BROWN
FOX JUMPS OVER A LAZY

ABCDEFGHIJKLMNOPQRSTU
VWXYZÄÇÉÑO123456789!?

the quick brown
fox jumps
over a lazy dog
lorem
ipsum dolor

Flat-it type foundry | www.flat-it.com

Gesso | Ryoichi Tsunekawa

THE QUICK BROWN

ABCDEFGHIJKLMNOPQRST
UVWXYZ0123456789&!?

Meegoreng | Ryoichi Tsunekawa

QUICK BROWN
FOX JUMPS OVER

ABCDEFGHIJKLMNOPQR
STUVWXYZ0123456789

Overwork | Ryoichi Tsunekawa

QUICK BROWN

ABCDEFGHIJKLMNOPQRS
TUVWXYZabcdefghijklmn
opqrstuvwxyz0123456789

| Palsu | Ryoichi Tsunekawa |

THE QUICK BROWN

ABCDEFGHIJKLMNOPQRS
TUVWXYZ0123456789!?

| Pusab | Ryoichi Tsunekawa |

BROWN FOX

ABCDEFGHIJKLMNOP
QRSTUVWXYZÄÇÉÑØ
0123456789(&:;!?$€)

| Plamo | Ryoichi Tsunekawa |

The quick brown fox jumps

ABCDEFGHIJKLMNOPQRSTUVW
XYZabcdefghijklmnopqrstu
vwxyz0123456789(&.,:!?$+%)

109

Sushitaro | Ryoichi Tsunekawa

イろハに示、ヘトチリヌハ

アイウえオカキワけこサシスセそ

たチッてトなにヌネのハヒフへ示、

まミムメモやュヨラリハれろワヲ

Tragedia | Ryoichi Tsunekawa

The quick brown

ABCDEFGHIJKLMNOP

QRSTUVWXYZabcdefghi

jklmnopqrstuvwxyz0123456789

Wood Stamp | Ryoichi Tsunekawa

FOX JUMPS OVER

ABCDEFGHIJKLMNOPQRSTUVWXYZABCDE

FGHIJKLMNOPQRSTUVWXYZ0123456789&

Fonthead Design Inc.

www.fonthead.com
support@fonthead.com

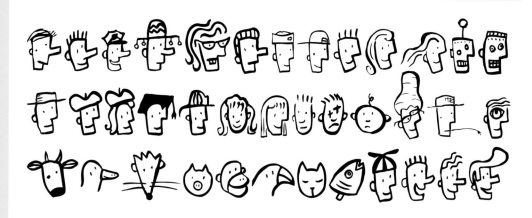

| Good Dog | Ethan Dunham |

The quick brown fox

ABCDEFGHIJKLMNOPQRSTUVWXY
Zabcdefghijklmnopqrstuvwxyz
äçéñöü0123456789($:;,!?$@)

| Good Dog Cool | Ethan Dunham |

The quick brown fox

ABCDEFGHIJKLMNOPQRSTUVWXY
Zabcdefghijklmnopqrstuvwxyz
äçéñöü0123456789($:;,!?$@)

Fonthead Design Inc. | www.fonthead.com

Holstein – Regular | Ethan Dunham

Quick brown fox jumps

ABCDEFGHIJKLMNOPQRSTUVWXY
Zabcdefghijklmnopqrstuvwxyzä
çéîñöüœ0123456789(&:;!?$£@)

Holstein – Bold | Ethan Dunham

Quick brown fox jumps

ABCDEFGHIJKLMNOPQRSTUVWXY
Zabcdefghijklmnopqrstuvwxyzä
çéîñöüœ0123456789(&:;!?$£@)

Millennia — Ethan Dunham

Brown Fox

ABCDEFGHIJKLMNOPQRST
UVWXYZabcdefghijklmno
pqrstuvwxyz0123456789

Red Five — Ethan Dunham

BROWN

ABCDEFGHIJKLM
NOPQRSTUVWX
YZ0123456789&

Smith Premier — Ethan Dunham

THE QUICK BROWN FOX JUMPS

AABCDEFGHIJKLMNOOPQRSTUV
WXYZ0123456789(:;!?$)

The quick brown fox JUMPS over a lazy dog Zwei Boxkämpfer

Fonthead Design Inc. | www.fonthead.com

Spill Milk | Ethan Dunham

The quick brown fox jumps over a

ABCDEFGHIJKLMNOPQRSTUVWXYZabcdefg

hijklmnopqrstuvwxyzäçéñö0123456789&!?

Tycho | Ethan Dunham

QUICK BROWN
FOX JUMPS OVER A

ABCDEFGHIJKLMN
OPQRSTUVWXYZ

Vladidmir | Ethan Dunham

QUICK BROWN
FOX JUMPS OVER A LAZY

ABCDEFGHIJkLMNOPQRSTUVWXYZ

Acme5 – Compressed | Nikos Giannakopoulos

ABCDEFGHIJKLMNOPQRSTU
VWXYZ0123456789!?ABГΔ
EZHΘIKΛMNΞOΠPΣTYΦXΨΩ

THE QUICK BROWN FOX JUMPS OVER A LAZY DOG. ZWEI BOXKÄMPFER JAGEN EVA
QUER DURCH SYLT. LOREM IPSUM DOLOR SIT AMET, CONSECTETUR ADIPISIC-
ING ELIT, SED DO EIUSMOD TEMPOR INCIDIDUNT UT LABORE ET DOLORE MAGNA
ALIQUA. THE QUICK BROWN FOX JUMPS OVER A LAZY DOG. ZWEI BOXKÄMPFER

Acme 5 – Wide | Nikos Giannakopoulos

ABCDEFGHIJKLMNOPQRSTUVWXY
Zabcdefghijklmnopqrstuvwxyzqčć
ñöŕśţüÜ0123456789(&:;!?$¢£¥€@)
ABГΔEZHΘIKΛMNΞOΠPΣTYΦXΨ
Ωαβγδεζηθικλμνξοπρσςτυφχψω

THE QUICK BROWN FOX jumps over a lazy dog. Zwei Boxkämpfer jagen Eva quer durch Sylt. Lorem ipsum dolor sit amet,
consectetur adipisicing elit, sed do eiusmod tempor incididunt
ut labore et dolore magna aliqua. The quick brown fox jumps

Acme 5 – Wide Bold | Nikos Giannakopoulos

ABCDEFGHIJKLMNOPQRSTUV
WXYZabcdefghijklmnopqrstu
vwxyz0123456789(&!?)ABГΔ
EZHΘIKΛMNΞOΠPΣTYΦXΨΩα
βγδεζηθικλμνξοπρσςτυφχψω

THE QUICK BROWN FOX jumps over a lazy dog. Zwei
Boxkämpfer jagen Eva quer durch Sylt. Lorem ipsum dolor sit amet, consectetur adipisicing elit, sed do eiusmod
tempor incididunt ut labore et dolore magna aliqua. The

ABCDEFGHIJKLMNOPQRSTUVWXY
Zabcdefghijklmnopqrstuvwxyząč
éïñøřśţüü0123456789(&.:;!?$¢£¥€)
ΑΒΓΔΕΖΗΘΙΚΛΜΝΞΟΠΡΣΤΥΦΧΨΩ
αβγδεζηθικλμνξοπρςτυφχψω

THE QUICK BROWN FOX jumps over a lazy dog. Zwei Boxkämpfer
jagen Eva quer durch Sylt. Lorem ipsum dolor sit amet, consectetur adipisicing elit, sed do eiusmod tempor incididunt ut labore

ABCDEFGHIJKLMNOPQRSTUV
WXYZabcdefghijklmnopqrstu
vwxyz0123456789(&!?)ABΓΔ
ΕΖΗΘΙΚΛΜΝΞΟΠΡΣΤΥΦΧΨΩα
βγδεζηθικλμνξοπρςτυφχψω

THE QUICK BROWN FOX jumps over a lazy dog. Zwei
Boxkämpfer jagen Eva quer durch Sylt. Lorem ipsum dolor sit amet, consectetur adipisicing elit, sed do eiusmod

ABCDEFGHIJKLMNOPQRSTUVWXYZabcde
fghijklmnopqrstuvwxyząčéïñøřşţü01234
56789(&.:;!?$¢£¥€)ABΓΔΕΖΗΘΙΚΛΜΝΞΟΠΡ
ΣΤΥΦΧΨΩαβγδεζηθικλμνξοπρςτυφχψω

THE QUICK BROWN FOX jumps over a lazy dog. Zwei
Boxkämpfer jagen Eva quer durch Sylt. Lorem ipsum
dolor sit amet, consectetur adipisicing elit, sed do

Acme 9 – Bold | Nikos Giannakopoulos

ABCDEFGHIJKLMNOPQRSTUVWXYZa
bcdefghijklmnopqrstuvwxyz012345
6789(&!?)ABΓΔΕΖΗΘΙΚΛΜΝΞΟΠΡΣΤΥ
ΦΧΨΩαβγδεζηθικλμνξοπρςτυφχψω

THE QUICK BROWN FOX jumps over a lazy dog. Zwei
Boxkämpfer jagen Eva quer durch Sylt. Lorem ipsum dolor sit amet, consectetur adipisicing elit,

Kyrou 5 – Wide | Nikos Giannakopoulos

ABCDEFGHIJKLMNOPQRSTUVWXY
Zabcdefghijklmnopqrstuvwxyzçč
áñöŕśţü0123456789(&:;!?$¢£¥€@)
ABΓΔΕΖΗΘΙΚΛΜΝΞΟΠΡΣΤΥΦΧΨΩ
αβγδεζηθικλμνξοπρςτυφχψω

THE QUICK BROWN FOX jumps over a lazy dog. Zwei Boxkämpfer
jagen Eva quer durch Sylt. Lorem ipsum dolor sit amet, consectetur adipisicing elit, sed do eiusmod tempor incididunt ut labore
et dolore magna aliqua. The quick brown fox jumps over a lazy

Kyrou 5 – Wide Bold | Nikos Giannakopoulos

ABCDEFGHIJKLMNOPQRSTUV
WXYZabcdefghijklmnopqrstu
vwxyz0123456789(&!?)ABΓΔ
ΕΖΗΘΙΚΛΜΝΞΟΠΡΣΤΥΦΧΨΩα
βγδεζηθικλμνξοπρςτυφχψω

THE QUICK BROWN FOX jumps over a lazy dog. Zwei
Boxkämpfer jagen Eva quer durch Sylt. Lorem ipsum dolor sit amet, consectetur adipisicing elit, sed do eiusmod
tempor incididunt ut labore et dolore magna aliqua. The

ABCDEFGHIJKLMNOPQRSTUVWX
YZabcdefghijklmnopqrstuvwxyz
ącéñoś0123456789(&::!?$¢£¥€@)
ΑΒΓΔΕΖΗΘΙΚΛΜΝΞΟΠΡΣΤΥΦΧΨΩ
αβγδεζηθικλμνξοπρςτυφχψω

THE QUICK BROWN FOX jumps over a lazy dog. Zwei Boxkämpfer
jagen Eva quer durch Sylt. Lorem ipsum dolor sit amet, consectetur adipisicing elit, sed do eiusmod tempor incididunt ut labore

ABCDEFGHIJKLMNOPQRSTUV
WXYZabcdefghijklmnopqrstu
vwxyz0123456789(&!?)ΑΒΓΔ
ΕΖΗΘΙΚΛΜΝΞΟΠΡΣΤΥΦΧΨΩα
βγδεζηθικλμνξοπρςτυφχψω

THE QUICK BROWN FOX jumps over a lazy dog. Zwei
Boxkämpfer jagen Eva quer durch Sylt. Lorem ipsum dolor sit amet, consectetur adipisicing elit, sed do eiusmod

ABCDEFGHIJKLMNOPQRSTUVWXYZabcde
fghijklmnopqrstuvwxyzącéñøśţü012345
6789(&::!?$¢£¥€@)ΑΒΓΔΕΖΗΘΙΚΛΜΝΞΟΠΡ
ΣΤΥΦΧΨΩαβγδεζηθικλμνξοπρςτυφχψω

THE QUICK BROWN FOX jumps over a lazy dog. Zwei
Boxkämpfer jagen Eva quer durch Sylt. Lorem ipsum dolor sit amet, consectetur adipisicing elit, sed do eiusmod

ABCDEFGHIJKLMNOPQRSTUVWXYZa
bcdefghijklmnopqrstuvwxyz012345
6789(&!?)ΑΒΓΔΕΖΗΘΙΚΛΜΝΞΟΠΡΣΤΥ
ΦΧΨΩαβγδεζηθικλμνξοπρςτυφχψω

THE QUICK BROWN FOX jumps over a lazy dog. Zwei
Boxkämpfer jagen Eva quer durch Sylt. Lorem ipsum dolor sit amet, consectetur adipisicing elit,

GUST e-foundry

www.gust.org.pl
b_jackowsk@gust.org.pl
janusz@jmn.pl
piotr@eps.gda.pl

Antykwa Półtawskiego – Regular | B. Jackowski, J.M. Nowacki, P. Strzelczyk

ABCDEFGHIJKLMNOPQRSTU
VWXYZabcdefghijklmnopqrst
uvwxyzącéñø0123456789(&:;!?)

THE QUICK BROWN FOX jumps over a lazy dog. Zwei Boxkämpfer jagen Eva quer
durch Sylt. Lorem ipsum dolor sit amet, consectetur adipisicing elit, sed do eiusmod
tempor incididunt ut labore et dolore magna aliqua. The quick brown fox jumps over

Antykwa Półtawskiego – Italic | B. Jackowski, J.M. Nowacki, P. Strzelczyk

ABCDEFGHIJKLMNOPQRSTU
VWXYZabcdefghijklmnopqrs
tuvwxyzącéñś0123456789(&:;!?)

*THE QUICK BROWN FOX jumps over a lazy dog. Zwei Boxkämpfer jagen Eva
quer durch Sylt. Lorem ipsum dolor sit amet, consectetur adipisicing elit, sed do
eiusmod tempor incididunt ut labore et dolore magna aliqua. The quick brown*

Antykwa Półtawskiego – Bold | B. Jackowski, J.M. Nowacki, P. Strzelczyk

**ABCDEFGHIJKLMNOPQRS
TUVWXYZabcdefghijklmn
opqrstuvwxyz0123456789&?**

**THE QUICK BROWN FOX jumps over a lazy dog. Zwei Boxkämpfer jagen
Eva quer durch Sylt. Lorem ipsum dolor sit amet, consectetur adipisicing
elit, sed do eiusmod tempor incididunt ut labore et dolore magna aliqua.**

The quick
brown
fox jumps over
a lazy dog
ZWEI
Boxkämpfer

GUST e-foundry | www.gust.org.pl

ABCDEFGHIJKLMNOPQRST UVWXYZabcdefghijklmnop qrstuvwxyząçé0123456789&!?

THE QUICK BROWN FOX jumps over a lazy dog. Zwei Boxkämpfer jagen Eva quer durch Sylt. Lorem ipsum dolor sit amet, consectetur adipisicing elit, sed do eiusmod tempor incididunt ut labore et dolore magna aliqua.

Igino Marini

www.iginomarini.com
iginomarini@yahoo.it

ABCDEFGHIJKLMNOPQR
STUVWXYZabcdefghijklmnop
qrstuvwxyząčéño123456789(&!?)

THE QUICK BROWN FOX jumps over a lazy dog. Zwei Boxkämpfer jagen Eva quer durch Sylt. Lorem ipsum dolor sit amet, consectetur adipisicing elit, sed do eiusmod tempor incididunt ut labore et dolore magna aliqua. The quick brown fox jumps over a lazy dog. Zwei Boxkämpfer

ABCDEFGHIJKLMNOPQR
STUVWXYZabcdefghijklmnopq
rstuvwxyząčéñoś123456789(&!?)

THE QUICK BROWN FOX jumps over a lazy dog. Zwei Boxkämpfer jagen Eva quer durch Sylt. Lorem ipsum dolor sit amet, consectetur adipisicing elit, sed do eiusmod tempor incididunt ut labore et dolore magna aliqua. The quick brown fox jumps over a lazy dog. Zwei Boxkämpfer jagen Eva quer durch Sylt.

ABCDEFGHIJKLMNOPQRS
TUVWXYZabcdefghijklmnopq
rstuvwxyząčéño123456789(&!?)

THE QUICK BROWN FOX jumps over a lazy dog. Zwei Boxkämpfer jagen Eva quer durch Sylt. Lorem ipsum dolor sit amet, consectetur adipisicing elit, sed do eiusmod tempor incididunt ut labore et dolore magna aliqua. Zwei Boxkämpfer

ABCDEFGHIJKLMNOPQR
STUVWXYZabcdefghijklmnopq
rstuvwxyząčéñøś0123456789(&!?)

THE QUICK BROWN FOX jumps over a lazy dog. Zwei Boxkämpfer jagen Eva quer durch Sylt. Lorem ipsum dolor sit amet, consectetur adipisicing elit, sed do eiusmod tempor incidunt ut labore et dolore magna aliqua. The quick brown fox jumps over a lazy dog. Zwei Boxkämpfer jagen Eva quer

ABCDEFGHIJKLMNOPQR
STUVWXYZabcdefghijklmno
pqrstuvwxyząčéñ0123456789(&!?)

THE QUICK BROWN FOX jumps over a lazy dog. Zwei Boxkämpfer jagen Eva quer durch Sylt. Lorem ipsum dolor sit amet, consectetur adipisicing elit, sed do eiusmod tempor incididunt ut labore et dolore magna aliqua. The quick brown fox jumps over a lazy dog. Zwei

ABCDEFGHIJKLMNOPQRST
UVWXYZabcdefghijklmnopqrstuv
wxyząčéñø0123456789(&!?$¢£¥€)

THE QUICK BROWN FOX jumps over a lazy dog. Zwei Boxkämpfer jagen Eva quer durch Sylt. Lorem ipsum dolor sit amet, consectetur adipisicing elit, sed do eiusmod tempor incidunt ut labore et dolore magna aliqua. The quick brown fox jumps over a lazy dog. Zwei Boxkämpfer jagen Eva quer durch

The quick
brown
fox jumps over
A LAZY DOG
Zwei Boxkämpfer
jagen Eva

IM FELL Flowers 1 & 2 | Igino Marini

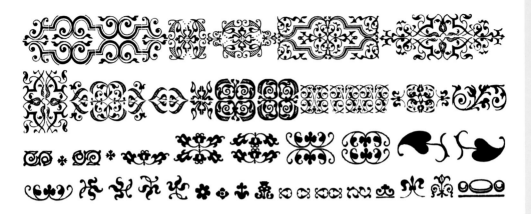

IM FELL French Canon Pro – Regular | Igino Marini

ABCDEFGHIJKLMNOPQRS TUVWXYZabcdefghijklmno pqrstuvwxyząčéo123456789&

THE QUICK BROWN FOX jumps over a lazy dog. Zwei Boxkämpfer jagen Eva quer durch Sylt. Lorem ipsum dolor sit amet, consectetur adipisicing elit, sed do eiusmod tempor incididunt ut labore et dolore magna aliqua. The quick brown fox jumps over a lazy dog.

IM FELL French Canon Pro – Italic | Igino Marini

ABCDEFGHIJKLMNOPQR STUVWXYZabcdefghijklmno pqrstuvwxyząčéo123456789&

THE QUICK BROWN FOX jumps over a lazy dog. Zwei Boxkämpfer jagen Eva quer durch Sylt. Lorem ipsum dolor sit amet, consectetur adipisicing elit, sed do eiusmod tempor incididunt ut labore et dolore magna aliqua. The quick brown fox jumps over a lazy dog. Zwei Boxkämp-

ABCDEFGHIJKLMNOPQRS TUVWXYZabcdefghijklmnopqr stuvwxyząčéñø0123456789(&!?)

THE QUICK BROWN FOX jumps over a lazy dog. Zwei Boxkämpfer jagen Eva quer durch Sylt. Lorem ipsum dolor sit amet, consectetur adipisicing elit, sed do eiusmod tempor incididunt ut labore et dolore magna aliqua. The quick brown fox jumps over a lazy dog. Zwei

ABCDEFGHIJKLMNOPQR STUVWXYZabcdefghijklmnopq rstuvwxyząčéñ0123456789(&!?)

THE QUICK BROWN FOX jumps over a lazy dog. Zwei Boxkämpfer jagen Eva quer durch Sylt. Lorem ipsum dolor sit amet, consectetur adipisicing elit, sed do eiusmod tempor incididunt ut labore et dolore magna aliqua. The quick brown fox jumps over a lazy dog. Zwei Boxkämpfer

QUICK BROWN FOX JUMPS OVER A LAZY

ABCDEFGHIJKLMNOPQRS TUVWXYZĄČÉĢÑØÜ(&:;!?)

Janusz Marian Nowacki

www.jmn.pl
janusz@jmn.pl

The quick
BROWN
fox jumps over a
lazy dog
Zwei Boxkämpfer
jagen Eva

Light

ABCDEFGHIJKLMNOPQRSTUVW
XYZabcdefghijklmnopqrstuvwxyz
0123456789(&:;!?$¢£¥€@)

Light Italic

ABCDEFGHIJKLMNOPQRSTUVW
XYZabcdefghijklmnopqrstuvwxyz
0123456789(&:;!?$¢£¥€@)

Regular

ABCDEFGHIJKLMNOPQRSTUV
WXYZabcdefghijklmnopqrstuvwx
yz0123456789(&:;!?$¢£¥€@)

Italic

ABCDEFGHIJKLMNOPQRSTUV
WXYZabcdefghijklmnopqrstuvwxy
z0123456789(&:;!?$¢£¥€@)

Medium

ABCDEFGHIJKLMNOPQRSTUV
WXYZabcdefghijklmnopqrstuvwx
yz0123456789(&:;!?$¢£¥€@)

Medium Condensed Italic

ABCDEFGHIJKLMNOPQRSTUVWX
YZabcdefghijklmnopqrstuvwxyz
0123456789(&:;!?$¢£¥€@)

Bold Condensed

ABCDEFGHIJKLMNOPQRSTUVW
XYZabcdefghijklmnopqrstuvwxyz
0123456789(&:;!?$¢£¥€@)

Bold Condensed Italic

ABCDEFGHIJKLMNOPQRSTUVW
XYZabcdefghijklmnopqrstuvwxyz
0123456789(&:;!?$¢£¥€@)

Heavy Condensed

ABCDEFGHIJKLMNOPQRSTUVW
XYZabcdefghijklmnopqrstuvwxyz
0123456789(&:;!?$¢£¥€@)

Heavy Condensed Italic

ABCDEFGHIJKLMNOPQRSTUVW
XYZabcdefghijklmnopqrstuvwxyz
0123456789(&:;!?$¢£¥€@)

La Tipomatika

www.tipomatika.co.nr
typomatika@gmail.com

Bruta Sans | Joan Alegret

The quick brown

ABCDEFGHIJKLMNOPQRST
UVWXYZabcdefghijklmno
pqrstuvwxyz0123456789!

New Cicle – Fina | Joan Alegret

ABCDEFGHIJKLMNOPQRSTUVW
XYZabcdefghijklmnopqrstuvwx
yzäçéîñü0123456789(&!?$¢£¥€)

THE QUICK BROWN FOX jumps over a lazy dog. Zwei Boxkämpfer jagen Eva quer durch Sylt.
Lorem ipsum dolor sit amet, consectetur adipisicing elit, sed do eiusmod tempor incididunt ut
labore et dolore magna aliqua. The quick brown fox jumps over a lazy dog. Zwei Boxkämpfer ja-

New Cicle – Fina Italic | Joan Alegret

ABCDEFGHIJKLMNOPQRSTUVW
XYZabcdefghijklmnopqrstuvwx
yzäçéîñü0123456789(&!?$¢£¥€)

THE QUICK BROWN FOX jumps over a lazy dog. Zwei Boxkämpfer jagen Eva quer durch Sylt.
Lorem ipsum dolor sit amet, consectetur adipisicing elit, sed do eiusmod tempor incididunt ut
labore et dolore magna aliqua. The quick brown fox jumps over a lazy dog. Zwei Boxkämpfer ja-

146

New Cicle – Semi | Joan Alegret

ABCDEFGHIJKLMNOPQRSTUVW
XYZabcdefghijklmnopqrstuvwx
yzäçéîñü0123456789(&!?$¢Ł¥€)

THE QUICK BROWN FOX jumps over a lazy dog. Zwei Boxkämpfer jagen Eva quer durch Sylt. Lorem ipsum dolor sit amet, consectetur adipisicing elit, sed do eiusmod tempor incididunt ut labore et dolore magna aliqua. The quick brown fox jumps over a lazy dog. Zwei Boxkämpfer ja-

New Cicle – Semi Italic | Joan Alegret

ABCDEFGHIJKLMNOPQRSTUVW
XYZabcdefghijklmnopqrstuvwx
yzäçéîñü0123456789(&!?$¢Ł¥€)

THE QUICK BROWN FOX jumps over a lazy dog. Zwei Boxkämpfer jagen Eva quer durch Sylt. Lorem ipsum dolor sit amet, consectetur adipisicing elit, sed do eiusmod tempor incididunt ut labore et dolore magna aliqua. The quick brown fox jumps over a lazy dog. Zwei Boxkämpfer ja-

New Cicle – Gordita | Joan Alegret

ABCDEFGHIJKLMNOPQRSTUVW
XYZabcdefghijklmnopqrstuvwx
yzäçéîñü0123456789(&!?$¢Ł¥€)

THE QUICK BROWN FOX jumps over a lazy dog. Zwei Boxkämpfer jagen Eva quer durch Sylt. Lorem ipsum dolor sit amet, consectetur adipisicing elit, sed do eiusmod tempor incididunt ut labore et dolore magna aliqua. The quick brown fox jumps over a lazy dog. Zwei Boxkämpfer ja-

New Cicle – Gordita Italic | Joan Alegret

ABCDEFGHIJKLMNOPQRSTUVW
XYZabcdefghijklmnopqrstuvwx
yzäçéîñü0123456789(&!?$¢£¥€)

THE QUICK BROWN FOX jumps over a lazy dog. Zwei Boxkämpfer jagen Eva quer durch Sylt.
Lorem ipsum dolor sit amet, consectetur adipisicing elit, sed do eiusmod tempor incididunt ut
labore et dolore magna aliqua. The quick brown fox jumps over a lazy dog. Zwei Boxkämpfer ja-

Simply Mono – Regular | Joan Alegret

BROWN FOX

ABCDEFGHIJKLM
NOPQRSTUVWXYZ
0123456789!?

Simply Mono – Oblique | Joan Alegret

BROWN FOX

ABCDEFGHIJKLM
NOPQRSTUVWXYZ
0123456789!?

Larabie Fonts

www.larabiefonts.com
typodermic@gmail.com

ABCDEFGHIJKLMNOPQRST
UVWXYZabcdefghijklmnopqrst
uvwxyząčéġñ0123456789(&!?€)

THE QUICK BROWN FOX jumps over a lazy dog. Zwei Boxkämpfer jagen Eva quer durch Sylt. Lorem ipsum dolor sit amet, consectetur adipisicing elit, sed do eiusmod tempor incididunt ut labore et dolore magna aliqua. The quick brown fox jumps over a lazy dog. Zwei

ABCDEFGHIJKLMNOPQRSTU
VWXYZabcdefghijklmnopqrstuvwx
yząčéġñøü0123456789(&:;!?$£¥€)

THE QUICK BROWN FOX jumps over a lazy dog. Zwei Boxkämpfer jagen Eva quer durch Sylt. Lorem ipsum dolor sit amet, consectetur adipisicing elit, sed do eiusmod tempor incididunt ut labore et dolore magna aliqua. The quick brown fox jumps over a lazy dog. Zwei Boxkämpfer jagen Eva quer

ABCDEFGHIJKLMNOPQRS
TUVWXYZabcdefghijklmnop
vwxyząčéġñ0123456789(&!?€)

THE QUICK BROWN FOX jumps over a lazy dog. Zwei Boxkämpfer jagen Eva quer durch Sylt. Lorem ipsum dolor sit amet, consectetur adipisicing elit, sed do eiusmod tempor incididunt ut labore et dolore magna aliqua. The quick brown fox jumps over a lazy

ABCDEFGHIJKLMNOPQRSTU
VWXYZabcdefghijklmnopqrstuvw
xyząčéġñø0123456789(&!?$£¥€)

THE QUICK BROWN FOX jumps over a lazy dog. Zwei Boxkämpfer jagen Eva quer durch Sylt. Lorem ipsum dolor sit amet, consectetur adipisicing elit, sed do eiusmod tempor incididunt ut labore et dolore magna aliqua. The quick brown fox jumps over a lazy dog. Zwei Boxkämpfer jagen Eva

The quick brown fox

ABCDEFGHIJKLMNOPQRSTUV
WXYZabcdefghijklmnopqrstu
vwxyząčéñ0123456789(&!?€)

Quick brown fox jumps

ABCDEFGHIJKLMNOPQRSTUVW
XYZabcdefghijklmnopqrstuvwxy
ząčéñöü0123456789(&;;!?$£¥€)

The quick brown fox

ABCDEFGHIJKLMNOPQRSTU
VWXYZabcdefghijklmnopqr
stuvwxyzączčé0123456789(€)

Quick brown fox jumps

ABCDEFGHIJKLMNOPQRSTUVW
XYZabcdefghijklmnopqrstuvwx
yzączčéñöşţü0123456789(&;;!?€)

Quick brown fox jumps

ABCDEFGHIJKLMNOPQRSTUVWXYZ
abcdefghijklmnopqrstuvwxyzäçé
0123456789(&;;!?$£¥€@)

The quick brown fox jumps

ABCDEFGHIJKLMNOPQRSTUVWXYZabcd efghijklmnopqrstuvwxyzäçéñöøšüœ 0123456789(&:;!?$£¥€@)

The quick brown fox

ABCDEFGHIJKLMNOPQRSTUVWXY Zabcdefghijklmnopqrstuvwxyz äçéñøø0123456789(&:;!?$£¥€@)

Quick brown fox jumps

ABCDEFGHIJKLMNOPQRSTUVWXYZab cdefghijklmnopqrstuvwxyzäçéñøü 0123456789(&:;!?$£¥€@)

153

ABCDEFGHIJKLMNOPQRSTUVWX YZabcdefghijklmnopqrstuvwxyzä çéñøüœ0123456789(&:;!?$¢¥€@)

THE QUICK BROWN FOX jumps over a lazy dog. Zwei Boxkämpfer jagen Eva quer durch Sylt. Lorem ipsum dolor sit amet, consectetur adipisicing elit, sed do eiusmod tempor incididunt ut labore et dolore magna aliqua. The quick brown fox jumps over a lazy dog. Zwei Boxkämpfer jagen Eva

ABCDEFGHIJKLMNOPQRSTUVWXYZ XYZabcdefghijklmnopqrstuvwxyzäçé 0123456789(&:;!?$¢¥€@)

THE QUICK BROWN FOX jumps over a lazy dog. Zwei Boxkämpfer jagen Eva quer durch Sylt. Lorem ipsum dolor sit amet, consectetur adipisicing elit, sed do eiusmod tempor incididunt ut labore et dolore magna aliqua. The quick brown fox jumps over a lazy dog. Zwei Boxkämpfer jagen Eva quer durch Sylt. Lorem ipsum dolor sit

ABCDEFGHIJKLMNOPQRSTUVW XYZabcdefghijklmnopqrstuvwx yzäçéñøü0123456789(&:;!?$€@)

THE QUICK BROWN FOX jumps over a lazy dog. Zwei Boxkämpfer jagen Eva quer durch Sylt. Lorem ipsum dolor sit amet, consectetur adipisicing elit, sed do eiusmod tempor incididunt ut labore et dolore magna aliqua. The quick brown fox jumps over a lazy dog. Zwei

Effloresce – Bold Italic | Ray Larabie

ABCDEFGHIJKLMNOPQRSTUVWXY
Zabcdefghijklmnopqrstuvwxyzäçé
0123456789(&:;!?$¥€@)

THE QUICK BROWN FOX jumps over a lazy dog. Zwei Boxkämpfer jagen Eva quer durch Sylt. Lorem ipsum dolor sit amet, consectetur adipisicing elit, sed do eiusmod tempor incididunt ut labore et dolore magna aliqua. The quick brown fox jumps over a lazy dog. Zwei Boxkämpfer jagen Eva quer

Goodfish – Regular | Ray Larabie

ABCDEFGHIJKLMNOPQRSTUVWX
YZabcdefghijklmnopqrstuvwxyzäçéñ
0123456789(&:;!?$¢£¥€@)

THE QUICK BROWN FOX jumps over a lazy dog. Zwei Boxkämpfer jagen Eva quer durch Sylt. Lorem ipsum dolor sit amet, consectetur adipisicing elit, sed do eiusmod tempor incididunt ut labore et dolore magna aliqua. The quick brown fox jumps over a lazy dog. Zwei Boxkämpfer jagen Eva quer durch

Goodfish – Italic | Ray Larabie

ABCDEFGHIJKLMNOPQRSTUVWXYZ
Zabcdefghijklmnopqrstuvwxyzäçéëñöøüœ
0123456789(&:;!?$¢£¥€@)

THE QUICK BROWN FOX jumps over a lazy dog. Zwei Boxkämpfer jagen Eva quer durch Sylt. Lorem ipsum dolor sit amet, consectetur adipisicing elit, sed do eiusmod tempor incididunt ut labore et dolore magna aliqua. The quick brown fox jumps over a lazy dog. Zwei Boxkämpfer jagen Eva quer durch Sylt. Lorem ipsum dolor sit amet,

ABCDEFGHIJKLMNOPQRSTUVW
XYZabcdefghijklmnopqrstuvwxyz
ãçéñøüæ0123456789(&:;!?$£¥€@)

THE QUICK BROWN FOX jumps over a lazy dog. Zwei Boxkämpfer jagen Eva quer durch Sylt. Lorem ipsum dolor sit amet, consectetur adipisicing elit, sed do eiusmod tempor incididunt ut labore et dolore magna aliqua. The quick brown fox jumps over a lazy dog. Zwei Boxkämpfer

ABCDEFGHIJKLMNOPQRSTUVWXY
Zabcdefghijklmnopqrstuvwxyzãçéñøü
0123456789(&:;!?$¢£¥€@)

THE QUICK BROWN FOX jumps over a lazy dog. Zwei Boxkämpfer jagen Eva quer durch Sylt. Lorem ipsum dolor sit amet, consectetur adipisicing elit, sed do eiusmod tempor incididunt ut labore et dolore magna aliqua. The quick brown fox jumps over a lazy dog. Zwei Boxkämpfer jagen Eva quer durch Sylt.

THE QUICK BROWN
ABCDEFGHIJKLMNOPQRSTU
VWXYZABCDEFGHIJKLMNOPQR
STUVWXYZĄČÉÑØ0123456789€

THE QUICK
BROWN
FOX JUMPS OVER
A LAZY DOG
ZWEI BOXKÄMPFER
JAGEN
EVA QUER DURCH

Kirsty – Italic   Ray Larabie

THE QUICK BROWN

ABCDEFGHIJKLMNOPQRSTUVW
YZABCDEFGHIJKLMNOPQRSTUVXYZĄ
ČÉĢÑØÜ0123456789(&:;!?$¢£¥€№)

Kirsty – Bold   Ray Larabie

THE QUICK BROWN

ABCDEFGHIJKLMNOPQRST
UVWXYZABCDEFGHIJKLMNOP
QRSTUVUVWXYZ0123456789

Kirsty – Bold Italic   Ray Larabie

THE QUICK BROWN

ABCDEFGHIJKLMNOPQRSTUV
WXYZABCDEFGHIJKLMNOPQRSTU
VWXYZĄČÉÑØ0123456789(&!?€)

158

ABCDEFGHIJKLMNOPQRSTUV WXYZabcdefghijklmnopqr stuvwxyzäçé0123456789€

THE QUICK BROWN FOX jumps over a lazy dog. Zwei Boxkämpfer jagen Eva quer durch Sylt. Lorem ipsum dolor sit amet, consectetur adipisicing elit, sed do eiusmod tempor incididunt ut labore et dolore magna aliqua. The quick brown

ABCDEFGHIJKLMNOPQRSTUVW XYZabcdefghijklmnopqrstuv wxyzäçéñ0123456789(&:;!?€)

THE QUICK BROWN FOX jumps over a lazy dog. Zwei Boxkämpfer jagen Eva quer durch Sylt. Lorem ipsum dolor sit amet, consectetur adipisicing elit, sed do eiusmod tempor incididunt ut labore et dolore magna aliqua. The quick brown fox jumps over a lazy dog.

ABCDEFGHIJKLMNOPQRSTUV WXYZabcdefghijklmnopqr stuvwxyzäçé0123456789€

THE QUICK BROWN FOX jumps over a lazy dog. Zwei Boxkämpfer jagen Eva quer durch Sylt. Lorem ipsum dolor sit amet, consectetur adipisicing elit, sed do eiusmod tempor incididunt ut labore et dolore magna aliqua. The quick brown

ABCDEFGHIJKLMNOPQRSTUVWX
YZabcdefghijklmnopqrstuvwx
yzäçéñ0123456789(&:;!?$¢£¥€)

THE QUICK BROWN FOX jumps over a lazy dog. Zwei Boxkämpfer jagen Eva quer durch Sylt. Lorem ipsum dolor sit amet, consectetur adipisicing elit, sed do eiusmod tempor incididunt ut labore et dolore magna aliqua. The quick brown fox jumps over a lazy dog. Zwei

ABCDEFGHIJKLMNOPQRSTU
VWXYZabcdefghijklmnop
qrstuvwxyz0123456789€

THE QUICK BROWN FOX jumps over a lazy dog. Zwei Boxkämpfer jagen Eva quer durch Sylt. Lorem ipsum dolor sit amet, consectetur adipisicing elit, sed do eiusmod tempor incididunt ut labore et dolore magna aliqua. The

ABCDEFGHIJKLMNOPQRSTUVW
XYZabcdefghijklmnopqrstuv
wxyzäçéî0123456789(&:;!?€)

THE QUICK BROWN FOX jumps over a lazy dog. Zwei Boxkämpfer jagen Eva quer durch Sylt. Lorem ipsum dolor sit amet, consectetur adipisicing elit, sed do eiusmod tempor incididunt ut labore et dolore magna aliqua. The quick brown fox jumps over a

Manfred Klein Fonteria

www.manfred-klein.ina-mar.com
petit11@t-online.de

ABCDEFGHIJKLMNOPQRSTU VWXYZabcdefghijklmnopqrst uvwxyzäçéñø0123456789(&!?€)

THE QUICK BROWN FOX jumps over a lazy dog. Zwei Boxkämpfer jagen Eva quer durch Sylt. Lorem ipsum dolor sit amet, consectetur adipisicing elit, sed do eiusmod tempor incididunt ut labore et dolore magna aliqua. The quick brown fox jumps over a lazy dog.

ABCDEFGHIJKLMNOPQRST UVWXYZabcdefghijklmnopqr stuvwxyzäçé0123456789&!?€

THE QUICK BROWN FOX jumps over a lazy dog. Zwei Boxkämpfer jagen Eva quer durch Sylt. Lorem ipsum dolor sit amet, consectetur adipisicing elit, sed do eiusmod tempor incididunt ut labore et dolore magna aliqua. The quick brown fox jumps over a lazy dog. Zwei

ABCDEFGHIJKLMNOPQRSTU VWXYZabcdefghijklmnopqrst uvwxyz0123456789(℧;;!?$¢£¥€)

THE QUICK BROWN FOX jumps over a lazy dog. Zwei Boxkämpfer jagen Eva quer durch Sylt Lorem ipsum dolor sit amet, consectetur adipisicing elit, sed do eiusmod tempor incididunt ut labore et dolore magna aliqua. The quick brown fox jumps over a lazy dog. Zwei Boxkämpfer jagen Eva

Chaplone | Manfred Klein

BROWN FOX JUMPS OVER A LAZY

ABCDEFGHIJKLMNOPQRS
TUVWXYZ0123456789!?€

DeconStruct – Light | Manfred Klein

ABCDEFGHIJKLMNOPQRSTUV
WXYZabcdefghijklmnopqrstuv
wxyzäçé0123456789(&!?$€)

THE QUICK BROWN FOX jumps over a lazy dog. Zwei Boxkämpfer jagen Eva quer durch Sylt. Lorem ipsum dolor sit amet, consectetur adipisicing elit, sed do eiusmod tempor incididunt ut labore et dolore magna aliqua. The quick brown fox jumps over a lazy dog. Zwei

DeconStruct – Light Oblique | Manfred Klein

ABCDEFGHIJKLMNOPQRSTUVW
XYZabcdefghijklmnopqrstuvwxy
zäçéñøü0123456789(&!?$Nº)

THE QUICK BROWN FOX jumps over a lazy dog. Zwei Boxkämpfer jagen Eva quer durch Sylt. Lorem ipsum dolor sit amet, consectetur adipisicing elit, sed do eiusmod tempor incididunt ut labore et dolore magna aliqua. The quick brown fox jumps over a lazy dog. Zwei Boxkämpfer

163

ABCDEFGHIJKLMNOPQRSTU VWXYZabcdefghijklmnopqrs tuvwxyz0123456789(&!?€№)

THE QUICK BROWN FOX jumps over a lazy dog. Zwei Boxkämpfer jagen Eva quer durch Sylt. Lorem ipsum dolor sit amet, consectetur adipisicing elit, sed do eiusmod tempor incididunt ut labore et dolore magna aliqua. The quick brown fox jumps over a lazy dog.

ABCDEFGHIJKLMNOPQRSTU VWXYZabcdefghijklmnopqrs tuvwxyz0123456789(&!?€№)

THE QUICK BROWN FOX jumps over a lazy dog. Zwei Boxkämpfer jagen Eva quer durch Sylt. Lorem ipsum dolor sit amet, consectetur adipisicing elit, sed do eiusmod tempor incididunt ut labore et dolore magna aliqua. The quick brown fox jumps over a lazy dog.

ABCDEFGHIJKLMNOPQRSTUVW XYZabcdefghijklmnopqrstuvwxyz äçéîñøüß0123456789(&:;!?$¢£¥€)

THE QUICK BROWN FOX jumps over a lazy dog. Zwei Boxkämpfer jagen Eva quer durch Sylt. Lorem ipsum dolor sit amet, consectetur adipisicing elit, sed do eiusmod tempor incididunt ut labore et dolore magna aliqua. The quick brown fox jumps over a lazy dog. Zwei Boxkämpfer

ABCDEFGHIJKLMNOPQRSTUVW
XYZabcdefghijklmnopqrstuvwxyz
äçéñøüß0123456789(&:;!?$¢£¥€)

THE QUICK BROWN FOX jumps over a lazy dog. Zwei Boxkämpfer jagen Eva quer durch Sylt. Lorem ipsum dolor sit amet, consectetur adipisicing elit, sed do eiusmod tempor incididunt ut labore et dolore magna aliqua. The quick brown fox jumps over a lazy dog. Zwei Boxkämpfer

ABCDEFGHIJKLMNOPQRSTUV
WXYZabcdefghijklmnopqrstu
vwxyzäçé0123456789(&:;!?€)

THE QUICK BROWN FOX jumps over a lazy dog. Zwei Boxkämpfer jagen Eva quer durch Sylt. Lorem ipsum dolor sit amet, consectetur adipisicing elit, sed do eiusmod tempor incididunt ut labore et dolore magna aliqua. The quick brown fox

ABCDEFGHIJKLMNOPQRSTU
VWXYZabcdefghijklmnopqrs
tuvwxyzäçéî0123456789&!?€

THE QUICK BROWN FOX jumps over a lazy dog. Zwei Boxkämpfer jagen Eva quer durch Sylt. Lorem ipsum dolor sit amet, consectetur adipisicing elit, sed do eius-mod tempor incididunt ut labore et dolore magna aliqua. The quick brown fox

The quick brown fox jumps over a lazy DOG

ABCDEFGHiJKLMNOPQRST UVWXYZabcdefghijklmnop qrstuvwxyz0123456789&!?

THE QUICK BROWN FOX jumps over a lazy dog. Zwei Boxkämpfer jagen Eva quer durch Sylt. Lorem ipsum dolor sit amet, consectetur adipisicing elit, sed do eiusmod tempor incididunt ut labore et dolore magna aliqua. The quick

ABCDEFGHIJKLMNOPQR STUVWXYZabcdefghijklmno pqrstuvwxyzäçé0123456789(&!?)

THE QUICK BROWN FOX jumps over a lazy dog. Zwei Boxkämpfer jagen Eva quer durch Sylt. Lorem ipsum dolor sit amet, consectetur adipisicing elit, sed do eiusmod tempor incididunt ut labore et dolore magna aliqua. The quick brown fox jumps over a lazy dog. Zwei Boxkämpfer

ABCDEFGHIJKLMNOPQR STUVWXYZABCDEFGHIJKL MNOPQRSTUVWXYZ0123456789!?

THE QUICK BROWN FOX JUMPS OVER A LAZY DOG. ZWEI BOXKÄMPFER JAGEN EVA QUER DURCH SYLT. LOREM IPSUM DOLOR SIT AMET, CONSECTETUR ADIPISICING ELIT, SED DO EIUSMOD TEMPOR INCIDIDUNT UT LABORE ET DOLORE MAGNA ALIQUA. THE QUICK BROWN

BROWN FOX

ABCDEFGHIJKLMNOPQRS
TUVWXYZabcdefghijklmn
opqrstuvwxyz0123456789&

ABCDEFGHIJKLMNOPQRST
UVWXYZabcdefghijklmnopq
rstuvwxyzäçé0123456789&!?

THE QUICK BROWN FOX jumps over a lazy dog. Zwei Boxkämpfer jagen Eva
quer durch Sylt. Lorem ipsum dolor sit amet, consectetur adipisicing elit, sed do
eiusmod tempor incididunt ut labore et dolore magna aliqua. The quick brown

ABCDEFGHIJKLMNOPQRS
TUVWXYZabcdefghijklmn
opqrstuvwxyz0123456789&

THE QUICK BROWN FOX jumps over a lazy dog. Zwei Boxkämpfer jagen
Eva quer durch Sylt. Lorem ipsum dolor sit amet, consectetur adipisicing
elit, sed do eiusmod tempor incididunt ut labore et dolore magna aliqua.

Latino Plain — Manfred Klein

ABCDEFGHIJKLMNOPQRSTU
VWXYZabcdefghijklmnopqr
qrstuvwxyzäçéñoı23456789&

THE QUICK BROWN FOX jumps over a lazy dog. Zwei Boxkämpfer jagen Eva quer durch Sylt. Lorem ipsum dolor sit amet, consectetur adipisicing elit, sed do eiusmod tempor incididunt ut labore et dolore magna aliqua. The quick brown fox jumps over

Near Aldus — Manfred Klein

ABCDEFGHIJKLMNOPQRSTUV
WXYZ*abcdefghijklmnopqrstuvwxyzäçé*
0123456789(& :;!?$)

THE QUICK BROWN FOX *jumps over a lazy dog. Zwei Boxkämpfer jagen Eva quer durch Sylt. Lorem ipsum dolor sit amet, consectetur adipisicing elit, sed do eiusmod tempor incididunt ut labore et dolore magna aliqua. The quick brown fox jumps over a lazy dog. Zwei Boxkämpfer jagen Eva quer durch Sylt. Lorem*

Ogi Rema Slabserif — Manfred Klein

ABCDEFGHIJKLMNOPQRSTUV
WXYZabcdefghijklmnopqrstuv
wxyzäçéñøü0123456789(&!?$€)

THE QUICK BROWN FOX jumps over a lazy dog. Zwei Boxkämpfer jagen Eva quer durch Sylt. Lorem ipsum dolor sit amet, consectetur adipisicing elit, sed do eiusmod tempor incididunt ut labore et dolore magna aliqua. The quick brown fox jumps over a lazy dog. Zwei Boxkämpfer ja-

ABCDEFGHIJKLMNOPQRSTUV WXYZabcdefghijklmnopqrstuv wxyzäçéñø0123456789(&!?$€)

THE QUICK BROWN FOX jumps over a lazy dog. Zwei Boxkämpfer jagen Eva quer durch Sylt. Lorem ipsum dolor sit amet, consectetur adipisicing elit, sed do eiusmod tempor incididunt ut labore et dolore magna aliqua. The quick brown fox jumps over a lazy dog.

ABCDEFGHIJKLMNOPQRSTU VWXYZabcdefghijklmnopqrstuv wyzäçéñøü0123456789(&!?$€)

THE QUICK BROWN FOX jumps over a lazy dog. Zwei Boxkämpfer jagen Eva quer durch Sylt. Lorem ipsum dolor sit amet, consectetur adipisicing elit, sed do eiusmod tempor incididunt ut labore et dolore magna aliqua. The quick brown fox jumps over a lazy dog. Zwei

ABCDEFGHIJKLMNOPQRSTUV WXYZabcdefghijklmnopqrstuvwxy zäçéñøüœstfi0123456789(&:;!?$)

THE QUICK BROWN FOX jumps over a lazy dog. Zwei Boxkämpfer jagen Eva quer durch Sylt. Lorem ipsum dolor sit amet, consectetur adipisicing elit, sed do eiusmod tempor incididunt ut labore et dolore magna aliqua. The quick brown fox jumps over a lazy dog. Zwei

ABCDEFGHIJKLMNOPQRST
UVWXYZabcdefghijklmnopqrst
uvwxyzäöüœqust0123456789(!?)

THE QUICK BROWN FOX jumps over a Lazy dog. Zwei Boxkämpfer jagen Eva quer durch Sylt. Lorem ipsum dolor sit amet, consectetur adipisicing elit, sed do eiusmod tempor incididunt ut Labore et dolore magna aliqua.

FOX JUMPS OVER

ABCDEFGHIJKLMNOPQRS
TUVWXYZabcdefghijklmn
opqrstuvwxyz0123456789&

ABCDEFGHIJKLMNOPQRSTU
VWXYZabcdefghijklmnopqrstu
vwxyzäçéñö0123456789($¢£¥)

THE QUICK BROWN FOX jumps over a lazy dog. Zwei Boxkämpfer jagen Eva quer durch Sylt. Lorem ipsum dolor sit amet, consectetur adipisicing elit, sed do eiusmod tempor incididunt ut labore et dolore magna aliqua. The quick brown fox jumps over a lazy dog.

ABCDEFGHIJKLMNOPQRST UVWXYZabcdefghijklmnop qrstuvwxyz0123456789&

THE QUICK BROWN FOX jumps over a lazy dog. Zwei Boxkämpfer jagen Eva quer durch Sylt. Lorem ipsum dolor sit amet, consectetur adipisicing elit, sed do eiusmod tempor incididunt ut labore et dolore magna aliqua. The

ABCDEFGHIJKLMNOPQRST UVWXYZabcdefghijklmnop qrstuvwxyz0123456789&

THE QUICK BROWN FOX jumps over a lazy dog. Zwei Boxkämpfer jagen Eva quer durch Sylt. Lorem ipsum dolor sit amet, consectetur adipisicing elit, sed do eiusmod tempor incididunt ut labore et dolore magna aliqua. The

ABCDEFGHIJKLMNOPQRSTU VWXYZabcdefghijklmnopqrstu vwxyzäçéîñ0123456789(&:;!?$€)

THE QUICK BROWN FOX jumps over a lazy dog. Zwei Boxkämpfer jagen Eva quer durch Sylt. Lorem ipsum dolor sit amet, consectetur adipisicing elit, sed do eiusmod tempor incididunt ut labore et dolore magna aliqua. The quick brown fox jumps over a lazy dog.

MartinPlus

www.martinplus.com
info@martinplus.com

ABCDEFGHIJKLMNOPQRSTUVWXYZabcdefg
hijklmnopqrstuvwxyz0123456789et!?£

THE QUICK BROWN FOX jumps over a lazy dog. Zwei Boxkämpfer jagen Eva
quer durch Sylt. Lorem ipsum dolor sit amet, consectetur adipisicing elit,
sed do eiusmod tempor incididunt ut labore et dolore magna aliqua. The

ABCDEFGHIJKLMNOPQRSTUVWXYZabcdef
ghijklmnopqrstuvwxyz0123456789!?£

THE QUICK BROWN FOX jumps over a lazy dog. Zwei Boxkämpfer jagen Eva
quer durch Sylt. Lorem ipsum dolor sit amet, consectetur adipisicing
elit, sed do eiusmod tempor incididunt ut labore et dolore magna ali-

ABCDEFGHIJKLMNOPQRSTUVWXYZabcde
fghijklmnopqrstuvwxyz0123456789

THE QUICK BROWN FOX jumps over a lazy dog. Zwei Boxkämpfer jagen Eva
quer durch Sylt. Lorem ipsum dolor sit amet, consectetur adipisicing
elit, sed do eiusmod tempor incididunt ut labore et dolore magna ali-

The quick brown

fox jumps

OVER A LAZY DOG

Zwei Boxkämpfer

Jagen Eva

Misprinted Type

www.misprintedtype.com
recife@misprintedtype.com

Astonished | Eduardo Recife

QUICK BROWN

ABCDEFGHIJKLMNOPQRSTUVWXYZab
cdefghijklmnopqrstuvwxyz0123456789

Dirty Ego | Eduardo Recife

QUICK BROWN

ABCDEFGHIJKLMNOPQRSTUVWXYZABCDE
FGHIJKLMNOPQRSTUVWXYZ0123456789&

Disgusting Behavior | Eduardo Recife

The quick brown fox jumps over

ABCDEFGHIJKLMNOPQRSTUVWX
YZabcdefghijklmnopqrstuvwxyzàçëñöüœ
0123456789(,;!?$€)

THE QUICK
BROWN
FOX JUMPS OVER A LAZY
DOG ZWEI
BOXKÄMPFER

Misproject | Eduardo Recife

QUICK BROWN

ABCDEFGHIJKLMNOPQRSTUVWXYZABCDE
FGHIJKLMNOPQRSTUVWXYZ0123456789ᴬᴺᴰ

Selfish | Eduardo Recife

The quick brown fox jumps

ABCDEFGHIJKLMN
OPQRSTUVWXYZabcdefghij
klmnopqrstuvwxyzäéñ0123456789(&!?)

Nick's Fonts

www.nicksfonts.com
himself@nicksfonts.com

The quick brown fox

ABCDEFGHIJKLMNOPQRST
UVWXYZabcdefghijklmnopqrstu
vwxyzäéñø0123456789(&:;!?$€)

Quick brown fox jumps

ABCDEFGHIJKLMNOPQRSTUV
WXYZabcdefghijklmnopqrstuvwxyzäé
îñøšüœ0123456789(&:;!?$¢£¥€@)

Quick brown fox jumps

ABCDEFGHIJKLMNOPQRSTUV
WXYZabcdefghijklmnopqrstuvwxyzäé
îñøšüœ0123456789(&:;!?$¢£¥€@)

quick brown fox jumps

abcdefghijklmnopqrstuvwxyz0123456789[&!?€]

ABCDEFGHIJKLMNOPQ
RSTUVWXYZabcdefghijkl
mnopqrstuvwxyz0123456789&

THE QUICK BROWN FOX jumps over a lazy dog. Zwei Boxkämpfer jagen Eva quer durch Sylt. Lorem ipsum dolor sit amet, consectetur adipisicing elit, sed do eiusmod tempor incididunt ut labore et dolore magna aliqua. The quick brown fox

The quick brown fox jumps

ABCDEFG HIJKLMNOPQR
STUVWXYZabcdefghijklmnopqrstuv
wxyzäçéîñøüœ0123456789(&::!?$¢£¥€)

183

BROWN FOX JUMPS

ABCDEFGHIJKLMNOPQRSTUVW
XYZABCDEFGHIJKLMNOPQRSTUVW
XYZÄÉÑØÜ0123456789[&:;!?$€]

The quick brown fox

ABCDEFGHIJKLMNOPQRSTUVWXYZ
abcdefghijklmnopqrstuvwxyzä
éîñøšü0123456789(&:;!?$¢£¥€@]

The quick brown fox jumps

ABCDEFGHIJKLMNOPQRSTUVW
XYZabcdefghijklmnopqrstuvwxyzä
éîñöøšüžœ0123456789[&:;!?$¢£¥€}

Quick brown
fox jumps over a lazy

ABCDEFGHIJKLMNOPQRST
UVWXYZabcdefghijklmno
pqrstuvwxyz0123456789&!?

ABCDEFGHIJKLMNOPQRST
UVWXYZabcdefghijklmnopqrstu
vwxyzäéñø0123456789(&:;!?$€)

THE QUICK BROWN FOX jumps over a lazy dog. Zwei Boxkämpfer jagen Eva quer durch
Sylt. Lorem ipsum dolor sit amet, consectetur adipisicing elit, sed do eiusmod tempor incididunt
ut labore et dolore magna aliqua. The quick brown fox jumps over a lazy dog. Zwei Boxkämpfer

Quick brown fox

ABCDEFGHIJKLMNOPQRSTUV
WXYZabcdefghijklmnopqrstuv
wxyzäéñø0123456789(&!?$€)

The quick brown

ABCDEFGHIJKLMNOPQ
RSTUVWXYZabcdefghijk
lmnopqrstuvwxyzäéñøüœ
0123456789(&:;!?$¢£¥€)

ABCDEFGHIJKLMNOPQ
RSTUVWXYZabcdefghijk
lmnopqrstuvwxyz0123456789

THE QUICK BROWN FOX jumps over a lazy dog. Zwei Boxkämpfer
jagen Eva quer durch Sylt. Lorem ipsum dolor sit amet, consectetur adipisicing elit, sed do eiusmod tempor incididunt ut labore et dolore magna

ABCDEFGHIJKLMNOPQ
RSTUVWXYZabcdefghijk
lmnopqrstuvwxyz0123456789

THE QUICK BROWN FOX jumps over a lazy dog. Zwei Boxkämpfer jagen Eva quer durch Sylt. Lorem ipsum dolor sit amet, consectetur adipisicing elit, sed do eiusmod tempor incididunt ut labore et do-

Lakeshore Drive NF | Nick Curtis

Brown fox

ABCDEFGHIJKLMNOPQRSTUVW
XYZabcdefghijklmnopq
rstuvwxyz0123456789&?

Materhorn NF | Nick Curtis

The quick brown

ABCDEFGHIJKLMNOPQRST
UVWXYZabcdefghijklmnopq
rstuvwxyz0123456789&!?

Mondo Redondo NF | Nick Curtis

the quick brown
fox jumps over a lazy

abcdefghijklmnopqrs
tuvwxyz0123456789ê!?

Orion Radio NF — Nick Curtis

QUICK BROWN

ABCDEFGHIJKLMN
OPQRSTUVWXYZÅ
0123456789(&₈₉!?1$€@)

Our Gang NF — Nick Curtis

Quick brown fox

ABCDEFGHIJKLMNOPQRSTUV
WXYZabcdefghijklmnopqrstuv
wxyzäéñø0123456789(&:;!?1€)

Park Lane NF — Nick Curtis

FOX JUMPS

ABCDEFGHIJKLMNOPQR
STUVWXYZ0123456789

Payzant Pen NF | Nick Curtis

Quick brown fox

ABCDEFGHIJKLMNOPQ
RSTUVWXYZabcdefghijkl
mnopqrstuvwxyz0123456789

Phatt Phreddy NF | Nick Curtis

Brown fox

ABCDEFGHIJKLMNOPQRST
UVWXYZabcdefghijklmn
opqrstuvwxyz0123456789

Ragg Mopp NF | Nick Curtis

JUMPS OVER

ABCDEFGHIJKLMNOPQR
STUVWXYZabcdefghijklm
nopqrstuvwxyz0123456789

189

The quick brown

ABCDEFGHIJKLMNOPQ
RSTUVWXYZabcdefghijkl
mnopqrstuvwxyz0123456789

The quick brown

ABCDEFGHIJKLMNOPQRS
TUVWXYZabcdefghijklmn
opqrstuvwxyz0123456789?

Quick brown

ABCDEFGHIJKLMNOPQRST
UVWXYZabcdefghijklmno
pqrstuvwxyz0123456789G

The quick
brown
fox jumps over
A LAZY DOG
Zwei Boxkämpfer
jagen

Two For Juan NF | Nick Curtis

BROWN FOX
JUMPS OVER A LAZY

ABCDEFGHIJKLMNOPQR
STUVWXYZ0123456789&

Underground NF | Nick Curtis

QUICK BROWN

ABCDEFGHIJKLMNOPQRST
UVWXYZABCDEFGHIJKLMNOP
QRSTUVWXYZ0123456789(&!?)

Uppen Arms NF | Nick Curtis

Quick brown

ABCDEFGHIJKLMNOPQRSTUV
WXYZabcdefghijklmnop
qrstuvwxyz0123456789&!?€

Objets Dart

www.objetsdart.ca
djrigby@gmail.com

ABCDEFGHIJKLMNOPQRSTUVW
XYZabcdefghijklmnopqrstuvwx
yząčéñø0123456789(&!?$€@)
АБВГДЕЁЖЗИЙКЛМНОПРСТУФ
ХЦЧШЩЪЫЬЭЮЯабвгдеёжзи
йклмнопрстуфхцчшщъыьэюя
ΑΒΓΔΕΖΗΘΙΚΛΜΝΞΟΠΡΣΤΥΦΧΨ
Ωαβγδεζηθικλμνξοπρσςτυφχψω

THE QUICK BROWN FOX jumps over a lazy dog. Zwei Boxkämpfer jagen Eva quer durch
Sylt. Lorem ipsum dolor sit amet, consectetur adipisicing elit, sed do eiusmod tempor
incididunt ut labore et dolore magna aliqua. The quick brown fox jumps over a lazy dog.
Zwei Boxkämpfer jagen Eva quer durch Sylt. Lorem ipsum dolor sit amet, consectetur

ABCDEFGHIJKLMNOPQRSTUVWXYZ
abcdefghijklmnopqrstuvwxyzäçéñ
0123456789(&:,!?$¢£¥€@)

THE QUICK BROWN FOX jumps over a lazy dog. Zwei Boxkämpfer jagen Eva quer durch Sylt.
Lorem ipsum dolor sit amet, consectetur adipisicing elit, sed do eiusmod tempor incididunt ut
labore et dolore magna aliqua. The quick brown fox jumps over a lazy dog. Zwei Boxkämpfer

Enigmatic – Bold | Darren Rigby

ABCDEFGHIJKLMNOPQRSTUVW XYZabcdefghijklmnopqrstuvw xyzäçé0123456789(&!?$€@)

THE QUICK BROWN FOX jumps over a lazy dog. Zwei Boxkämpfer jagen Eva quer durch Sylt. Lorem ipsum dolor sit amet, consectetur adipisicing elit, sed do eiusmod tempor incididunt ut labore et dolore magna aliqua. The quick brown fox jumps

Hindsight (Unicode) – Regular | Darren Rigby

ABCDEFGHIJKLMNOPQRSTUVWX YZabcdefghijklmnopqrstuvw xyząčé0123456789(&:;!?$£Ÿ€) АБВГДЕЁЖЗИЙКЛМНОПРСТУФХ ЦЧШЩЪЫЬЭЮЯабвгдеёжзий клмнопрстуфхцчшщъыьэюя ΑΒΓΔΕΖΗΘΙΚΛΜΝΞΟΠΡΣΥΦΧΨΩα βγδεζηθικλμνξοπρςστυφχψω

THE QUICK BROWN FOX jumps over a lazy dog. Zwei Boxkämpfer jagen Eva quer durch Sylt. Lorem ipsum dolor sit amet, consectetur adipisicing elit, sed do eiusmod tempor incididunt ut labore et dolore magna aliqua. The quick brown fox jumps over a lazy dog. Zwei Boxkämpfer jagen Eva quer durch

ABCDEFGHIJKLMNOPQRSTUVWXYZ

abcdefghijklmnopqrstuvwxyzä

çéñøšü0123456789(&:;!?$¢£¥€)

THE QUICK BROWN FOX jumps over a lazy dog. Zwei Boxkämpfer jagen Eva quer durch Sylt. Lorem ipsum dolor sit amet, consectetur adipisicing elit, sed do eiusmod tempor incididunt ut labore et dolore magna aliqua. The quick brown fox jumps

ABCDEFGHIJKLMNOPQRSTUVWX

YZABCDEFGHIJKLMNOPQRSTUVW

XYZÄÇÉÑ0123456789(&!?$£¥€)

THE QUICK BROWN FOX JUMPS OVER A LAZY DOG. ZWEI BOXKÄMPFER JAGEN EVA QUER DURCH SYLT. LOREM IPSUM DOLOR SIT AMET, CONSECTETUR ADIPISICING ELIT, SED DO EIUSMOD TEMPOR INCIDIDUNT UT LABORE ET DOLORE MAGNA ALIQUA. THE QUICK BROWN

QUICK BROWN

ABCDEFGHIJKLM

NOPQRSTUVWXY

Z0123456789(&!?)

Quick brown

ABCDEFGHIJKLMNOPQRS
TUVWXYZabcdefghijklmno
pqrstuvwxyz0123456789&

ABCDEFGHIJKLMNOPQRSTUVWXYZab
cdefghijklmnopqrstuvwxyzäçéíñøü
0123456789(&:;!?$¢£¥€)

THE QUICK BROWN FOX jumps over a lazy dog. Zwei Boxkämpfer jagen Eva quer durch Sylt. Lorem ipsum dolor sit amet, consectetur adipisicing elit, sed do eiusmod tempor incididunt ut labore et dolore
magna aliqua. The quick brown fox jumps over a lazy dog. Zwei Boxkämpfer jagen Eva quer durch

ABCDEFGHIJKLMNOPQRSTUVWXYZab
cdefghijklmnopqrstuvwxyzäçéñ
0123456789(&:;!?$¢£¥€)

THE QUICK BROWN FOX jumps over a lazy dog. Zwei Boxkämpfer jagen Eva quer durch
Sylt. Lorem ipsum dolor sit amet, consectetur adipisicing elit, sed do eiusmod
tempor incididunt ut labore et dolore magna aliqua. The quick brown fox jumps over

197

ABCDEFGHIJKLMNOPQRST
UVWXYZabcdefghijklmnop
qrstuvwxyz0123456789(&!?)

THE QUICK BROWN FOX jumps over a lazy dog. Zwei Boxkämpfer jagen Eva quer durch Sylt. Lorem ipsum dolor sit amet, consectetur adipisicing elit, sed do eiusmod tempor incididunt ut labore et dolore magna aliqua. The quick

LAZY DOG

ABCDEFGHIJKLMNOPQRSTU
VWXYZabcdefghijklmnop
qrstuvwxyz0123456789

quick brown fox jumps over

ABCDEFGHIJKLMNOPQRSTUVWXYZ
abcdefghijklmnopqrstuvwxyz
0123456789(&:;!?$@)

Three-Sixty   Darren Rigby

Quick brown

ABCDEFGHIJKLMNOPQRST
UVWXYZabcdefghijklmno
pqrstuvwxyz0123456789

Three-Sixty Condensed   Darren Rigby

The quick brown

ABCDEFGHIJKLMNOPQRSTU
VWXYZabcdefghijklmnopq
rstuvwxyz0123456789&!?

Tin Birdhouse – Regular   Darren Rigby

ABCDEFGHIJKLMNOPQRSTUVW
XYZabcdefghijklmnopqrstuvw
xyzäçéñ0123456789(&!?€@)

THE QUICK BROWN FOX jumps over a lazy dog. Zwei Boxkämpfer jagen Eva quer durch Sylt.
Lorem ipsum dolor sit amet, consectetur adipisicing elit, sed do eiusmod tempor incididunt ut labore et dolore magna aliqua. The quick brown fox jumps over a lazy dog. Zwei

ABCDEFGHIJKLMNOPQRSTUVWXY
Zabcdefghijklmnopqrstuvwxyzä
çéñøü0123456789(&:;!?Şċ£¥€@)

THE QUICK BROWN FOX jumps over a lazy dog. Zwei Boxkämpfer jagen Eva quer durch Sylt. Lorem ipsum dolor sit amet, consectetur adipisicing elit, sed do eiusmod tempor incididunt ut labore et dolore magna aliqua. The quick brown fox jumps over a lazy dog. Zwei Boxkämpfer

ABCDEFGHIJKLMNOPQRSTUVW
XYZabcdefghijklmnopqrstuvw
xyzäçéî0123456789(&:;!?Ş€)

THE QUICK BROWN FOX jumps over a lazy dog. Zwei Boxkämpfer jagen Eva quer durch Sylt. Lorem ipsum dolor sit amet, consectetur adipisicing elit, sed do eiusmod tempor incididunt ut labore et dolore magna aliqua. The quick brown fox jumps over a lazy dog.

ABCDEFGHIJKLMNOPQRSTUVWXY
Zabcdefghijklmnopqrstuvwxyzä
çéîñø0123456789(&:;!?Şċ£¥€@)

THE QUICK BROWN FOX jumps over a lazy dog. Zwei Boxkämpfer jagen Eva quer durch Sylt. Lorem ipsum dolor sit amet, consectetur adipisicing elit, sed do eiusmod tempor incididunt ut labore et dolore magna aliqua. The quick brown fox jumps over a lazy dog. Zwei Boxkämpfer

pizzadude.dk

www.freefonts.pizzadude.dk
jakob@pizzadude.dk

Quick brown fox jumps

ABCDEFGHIJKLMNOPQRSTUVWXYZ
abcdefghijklmnopqrstuvwxyzåøæ
0123456789(&:;!?$€£¥@)

BROWN FOX

ABCDEFGHIJKLMNOPQRSTU
VWXYZABCDEFGHIJKLMNOP
QRSTUVWXYZ0123456789(&:;!?)

The quick brown

ABCDEFGHIJKLMNOPQRSTUV
WXYZabcdefghijklmnopqrstuv
wxyz0123456789(&.,:;!?$©)

Blatant — Jakob Fischer

THE QUICK BROWN FOX JUMPS OVER A DOG

ABCDEFGHIJKLMNOPQR
STUVWXYZ0123456789

Blindfold — Jakob Fischer

The quick brown

ABCDEFGH I JKLMNOPQRS
TUVWXYZabcdefghijklmnop
qrstuvwxyzåø0123456789(;:!?)

Crosspatchers Delight Normal — Jakob Fischer

THE QUICK BROWN FOX JUMPS

ABCDEFGHIJKLMNOPQRSTUVWXYZ
abcdefghijklmnopqrstuvwxyzäéíñøü
0123456789(&.,:;!?$@)

203

Crosspatchers Delight   Jakob Fischer

The quick brown fox jumps over

ABCDEFGHIJKLMNOPQRSTUVWXYZ

abcdefghijklmnopqrstuvwxyzäéñöøü

0123456789(&:;!?$£@)

Fazings One   Jakob Fischer

Flashit   Jakob Fischer

QUICK BROWN

ABCDEFGHIJKLMNOPQ
RSTUVWXYZABCDEFGH
IJKLMNOPQRSTUVWXY
ZÅØÆ0123456789(:;!?€)

The quick brown fox jumps

ABCDEFGHIJKLMNOPQRSTUVWXYZ
abcdefghijklmnopqrstuvwxyzåøα
0123456789(&:;!?$&@)

Quick brown fox jumps over a

ABCDEFGHIJKIMNOPQRSTUVWXYZ
abcdefghijklmnopqrstuvwxyzåøßæ
0123456789(&:;!?$¢€£@)

BROWN FOX

ABCDEFGHIJKLMNOPQRSTU
VWXYZABCDEFGHIJKLMNOP
QRSTUVWXYZ0123456789&

pizzadude.dk | www.freefonts.pizzadude.dk

Quick brown

ABCDEFGHIJKLMNOPQRST
UVWXYZabcdefghijklmnopq
rstuvwxyz0123456789&::!?$@

Idolwild | Jakob Fischer

Quick brown

ABCDEFGHIJKLMNOPQRST
UVWXYZabcdefghijklmno
pqrstuvwxyz0123456789&

Joint By Pizzadude | Jakob Fischer

Quick brown

ABCDEFGHIJKLMNOPQRST
UVWXYZabcdefghijklmnop
qrstuvwxyz0123456789&$

The quick brown fox jumps over a lazy DOG Lorem ipsum

pizzadude.dk | www.freefonts.pizzadude.dk

Just A Dream Solid — Jakob Fischer

QUICK BROWN

ABCDEFGHIJKLMNOPQRSTUV
WXYZABCDEFGHIJKLMNOPQ
RSTUVWXYZO123456789&

Just A Dream Hollow — Jakob Fischer

QUICK BROWN

ABCDEFGHIJKLMNOPQRSTUV
WXYZABCDEFGHIJKLMNOPQ
RSTUVWXYZO123456789&

Love Letters — Jakob Fischer

The quick brown fox

ABCDEFGHIJKLMNOPQRSTUVW
XYZabcdefghijklmnopqrs
tuvwxyz0123456789($)

the quick brown fox

ABCDEFGHiJKLMNOPQRSTUV
WXYZabcdefghijklmnopqrs
tuvwxyz0123456789(!?)

THE QUICK BROWN

ABCDEFGHIJKLMNOPQRSTUV
WXYZÄÇÉÑØ0123456789(!?)

QUICK BROWN FOX

ABCDEFGHIJKLMNOP
QRSTUVWXYZÅØÆ
0123456789(&;:!?$@)

Schoolbully | Jakob Fischer

QUICK BROWN FOX JUMPS

ABCDEFGHIJKLMNOPQRSTUVWXYZABCDE
FGHIJKLMNOPQRSTUVWXYZÄÇÉÎÑÖØÜÆ
0123456789(&:;!?$¢€£¥@)

Squareheads | Jakob Fischer

Tags Xtreme 2 | Jakob Fischer

the QUICK bROWN fox

ABCDEFGHIJKLMNOPQRSTUVWXY
Zabcdefghijklmnopqrstuvw
xyz0123456789(&:;!?$@✪)

210

The quick brown

ABCDEFGHIJKLMNOPQRSTU
VWXYZabcdefghijklmnopqrst
uvwxyz0123456789(&!?$@)

THE QUICK BROWN FOX

aBCDEFGHIJKLMNOPQRStuvwXYZaBCDE
FGHIJKLMNOPQRStuvwXY20123456789$

THE QUICK BROWN

ABCDEFGHIJKLMNOPQRSTU
VWXYZABCDEFGHIJKLMNOPQ
RSTUVWXYZ0123456789!?

THE QUICK BROWN
FOX JUMPS OVER A LAZY

ABCDEFGHIJKLMNOPQRSTU
VWXYZÄÉÑØ0123456789(&!?@)

QUICK BROWN FOX JUMPS

ABCDEFGHIJKLMNOPQRSTUVWXYZabcdefg
hijklmnopqrstuvwxyz0123456789(&!?)

BROWN FOX

ABCDEFGHIJKLMNOPQRST
UVWXYZ0123456789&:;!?

Reading Type

www.readingtype.org.uk
ben@readingtype.org.uk

Acknowledgement | Ben Weiner

BROWN

ABCDEFGHIJKLM NOPQRSTUVWXY Z0123456789&:;!?

Bentham | Ben Weiner

ABCDEFGHIJKLMNOPQRS TUVWXYZabcdefghijklmno pqrstuvwxyz0123456789&!?

THE QUICK BROWN FOX jumps over a lazy dog. Zwei Boxkämpfer jagen Eva quer durch Sylt. Lorem ipsum dolor sit amet, consectetur adipisicing elit, sed do eiusmod tempor incididunt ut labore et dolore magna aliqua. The quick brown

Geo – Regular | Ben Weiner

ABCDEFGHIJKLMNOPQRSTUV WXYZabcdefghijklmnopqrs tuvwxyz0123456789[&:;!?]

THE QUICK BROWN FOX jumps over a lazy dog. Zwei Boxkämpfer jagen Eva quer durch Sylt. Lorem ipsum dolor sit amet, consectetur adipisicing elit, sed do eiusmod tempor incididunt ut labore et dolore magna aliqua. The quick brown fox jumps over a

The quick BROWN fox jumps over a lazy dog

Zwei Boxkämpfer jagen Eva

ABCDEFGHIJKLMNOPQRSTUV
WXYZabcdefghijklmnopqrs
tuvwxyz0123456789[&!?]

THE QUICK BROWN FOX jumps over a lazy dog. Zwei Boxkämpfer jagen Eva quer durch Sylt. Lorem ipsum dolor sit amet, consectetur adipisicing elit, sed do eiusmod tempor incididunt ut labore et dolore magna aliqua. The quick brown fox jumps over a

ABCDEFGHIJKLMNOPQRSTUVW
XYZabcdefghijklmnopqrstuvw
xyzäéño123456789(&!?$£¥€)

THE QUICK BROWN FOX jumps over a lazy dog. Zwei Boxkämpfer jagen Eva quer durch Sylt. Lorem ipsum dolor sit amet, consectetur adipisicing elit, sed do eiusmod tempor incididunt ut labore et dolore magna aliqua. The quick brown fox jumps over a lazy dog. Zwei

ABCDEFGHIJKLMNOPQRSTUVW
XYZabcdefghijklmnopqrstuvw
xyzäéño123456789(&!?$£¥€)

THE QUICK BROWN FOX jumps over a lazy dog. Zwei Boxkämpfer jagen Eva quer durch Sylt. Lorem ipsum dolor sit amet, consectetur adipisicing elit, sed do eiusmod tempor incididunt ut labore et dolore magna aliqua. The quick brown fox jumps over a lazy dog. Zwei

ABCDEFGHIJKLMNOPQRSTUVW
XYZabcdefghijklmnopqrstuvw
xyzäéñ0123456789(&!?$£¥€)

THE QUICK BROWN FOX jumps over a lazy dog. Zwei Boxkämpfer jagen Eva quer durch Sylt. Lorem ipsum dolor sit amet, consectetur adipisicing elit, sed do eiusmod tempor incididunt ut labore et dolore magna aliqua. The quick brown fox jumps over a lazy dog. Zwei

ABCDEFGHIJKLMNOPQRSTUVW
XYZabcdefghijklmnopqrstuvw
xyzäéñ0123456789(&!?$£¥€)

THE QUICK BROWN FOX jumps over a lazy dog. Zwei Boxkämpfer jagen Eva quer durch Sylt. Lorem ipsum dolor sit amet, consectetur adipisicing elit, sed do eiusmod tempor incididunt ut labore et dolore magna aliqua. The quick brown fox jumps over a lazy dog. Zwei

ABCDEFGHIJKLMNOPQRSTUVWX
YZabcdefghijklmnopqrstuvwxy
zäéíñü0123456789(&:;!?$¢£¥€)

THE QUICK BROWN FOX jumps over a lazy dog. Zwei Boxkämpfer jagen Eva quer durch Sylt. Lorem ipsum dolor sit amet, consectetur adipisicing elit, sed do eiusmod tempor incididunt ut labore et dolore magna aliqua. The quick brown fox jumps over a lazy dog. zwei boxkämpfer jagen eva

ABCDEFGHIJKLMNOPQRSTUVWX YZabcdefghijklmnopqrstuvwxy zäéñü0123456789(&:;!?$¢£¥€)

THE QUICK BROWN FOX jumps over a lazy dog. Zwei Boxkämpfer jagen Eva quer durch Sylt. Lorem ipsum dolor sit amet, consectetur adipisicing elit, sed do eiusmod tempor incididunt ut labore et dolore magna aliqua. The quick brown fox jumps over a lazy dog. zwei boxkämpfer jagen eva

Rob Meek

www.robmeek.com
ffi@robmeek.com

minimeek | Rob Meek

BROWN FOX

ABCDEFGHIJKLMNOPQRSTU
UVWXYZabcdefghijklmnopq
rstuvwxyz0123456789&!?

Modular Nouveau No.2 | Rob Meek

the quick brown

ABCDEFGHIJKLMNOPQRSTUVW
XYZabcdefghijklmnopqrstu
vwxyzäçé0123456789(&!?(a))

Snipped | Rob Meek

brown fox

ABCDEFGHIJKLMNOPQRSTU
VWXYZabcdefghijklmnop
qrstuvwxyz0123456789€

THE QUICK
BROWN
FOX JUMPS OVER
A LAZY DOG
ZWEI
BOXKÄMPFER
JAGEN EVA

The quick brown

ABCDEFGHIJKLMNOPQRSTUVW
XYZabcdefghijklmnopqrstuvw
xyzäçéÜ0123456789(&:;!?$€®)

Shamfonts

www.shamfonts.com
shamfonts@shamrocking.com

Freshco | Shamrock

The quick brown

ABCDEFGHIJKLMNOPQRSTUVWXYZ
abcdefghijklmnopqrstuvwxyz0123456789

Putain | Shamrock

Brown fox jumps over

ABCDEFGHIJKLMNOPQRS
TUVWXYZabcdefghijklmnop
qrstuvwxyzäçéñ0123456789&

Sham Block | Shamrock

QUICK BROWN FOX JUMPS

AABBCCDDEEFFGGHHIIJJKKLLMMN
NOOPPQQRRSSTTUUVVWWXXYYZZ

THE QUICK BROWN
FOX JUMPS
OVER A LAZY DOG

UC&LC   SHAMROCK
                 SHAM-
                 BLOCK

ALTERNATE SHIFT WHILE TYPING

SHIFT

Illustration © 2008 Shamrock int.

225

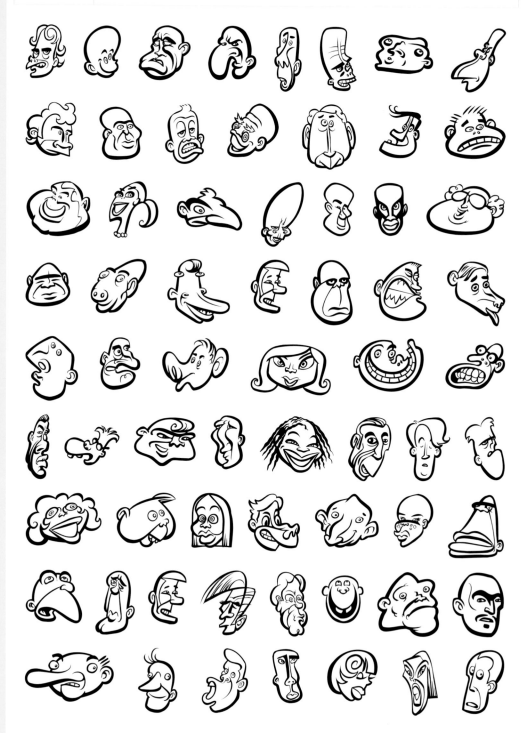

SMeltery | www.smeltery.net

Regular

ABCDEFGHIJKLMNOPQRSTUVWXY
Zabcdefghijklmnopqrstuvwxyzä
çéîñøü0123456789(&:;!?ə)

Italic

ABCDEFGHIJKLMNOPQRSTUVWXY
Zabcdefghijklmnopqrstuvwxyzä
çéîñøü0123456789(&:;!?ə)

Bold

ABCDEFGHIJKLMNOPQRSTUVWXY
Zabcdefghijklmnopqrstuvwxyzä
çéîñøü0123456789(&:;!?ə)

Bold Italic

ABCDEFGHIJKLMNOPQRSTUVWXY
Zabcdefghijklmnopqrstuvwxyzä
çéîñøü0123456789(&:;!?ə)

THE QUICK BROWN FOX jumps over a lazy dog. Zwei Boxkämpfer jagen Eva quer durch Sylt. Lorem ipsum dolor sit amet, consectetur adipisicing elit, sed do eiusmod tempor incididunt ut labore et dolore magna aliqua. The quick brown fox jumps over a lazy dog. Zwei Boxkämpfer

The quick
BROWN
fox jumps over
a lazy dog
Zwei Boxkämpfer
jagen Eva

BAnkrutt | Jack Usine

Quick brown

ABCDEFGHIJKLMNOPQRSTU
VWXYZabcdefghijklmnopq
rstuvwxyz☉0123456789(&:;!?)

STigmate | Jack Usine

Quick brown fox jumps

ABCDEFGHIJKLMNOPQRSTUV
WXYZabcdefghijklmnopqrstuv
wxyzäçéñøü0123456789(&:;!?)

TRottoir | Jack Usine

JUMPS OVER

ABCDEFGHIJKLMNOPQ
RSTUVWXYZABCDEFGHIJ
KLMNOPQRSTUVWXYZÄÇÉÑØ
0123456789[&:;!?$¢£¥€]

Sonntag Fonts

www.sonntag.nl
info@sonntag.nl

35

01234

56789

Selfism – Regular | Jan Sonntag

quick brown fox jumps

ABCDEFGHIJKLMNOPQRSTUVWXY
zabcdefghijklmnopqrstuvwx
yzäçéñøß0123456789[&!.?$£¥€@]

Selfism – Bold | Jan Sonntag

the quick brown fox

ABCDEFGHIJKLMNOPQRSTUVWX
yzabcdefghijklmnopqrstuvw
xyzäçéñøß0123456789[&!.?$€@]

Spijner – Regular (selection) | Jan Sonntag

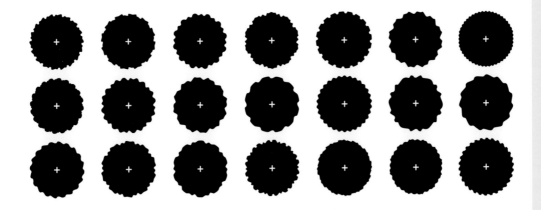

233

The quick
brown
fox jumps over
a lazy dog
ZWEI

Takraf – Block | Jan Sonntag

QUICK BROWN

ABCDEFGHIJKLM
NOPQRSTUVWXYZ
0123456789

Takraf – Linie | Jan Sonntag

QUICK BROWN

ABCDEFGHIJKLM
NOPQRSTUVWXYZ
0123456789

Takraf – VEB | Jan Sonntag

BROWN FOX

ABCDEFGHIJKLM
NOPQRSTUVWXYZ
0123456789

Typedifferent

www.typedifferent.com
typedifferent@burodestruct.net

BD Alm | Büro Destruct

QUICK BROWN FOX JUMPS

abcdefghijklmnopqrstuvwxyz
abcdefghijklmnopqrstuvwxy
zäöü0123456789(&;;!?$)

BD Bardust | Büro Destruct

the quick brown
fox jumps over a lazy

abcdefghijklmnopqrstu
vwxyzäéîöö0123456789!?

BD Beans | Büro Destruct

brown fox
jumps over a lazy

AbCdEFGHIJKLMNOPQRS
TUVWXYZ0123456789(!?)

BD Bill Ding | Büro Destruct

The quick brown

ABCDEFGHIJKLMNOPQRSTU
VWXYZabcdefghijklmnop
qrstuvwxyz0123456789!?

BD Bill Ding – Long | Büro Destruct

brown

BD Billiet | Büro Destruct

The quick brown fox

ABCDEFGHIJKLMNOPQRSTUVWX
YZabcdefghijklmnopqrstuvwx
yzäçéîöü0123456789(&:;!?$£)

239

BD Burner | Büro Destruct

Quick brown

ABCDEFGHIJKLMNOPQRS
TUVWXYZabcdefghijklmnop
qrstuvwxyz0123456789g(&(?)

BD Console | Büro Destruct

brown

JUMPS OVER A LAZY

ABCDEFGHIJKLMNOPQ
RSTUVWXYZ0123456789@@

BD Console Remix | Büro Destruct

quick brown

ABCDEFGHIJKLMNOPQ
RSTUVWXYZabcdefg
hijklmnopqrstuvwx
yzäöéüü0123456789@!?@

THE QUICK
BROWN
FOX JUMPS OVER
A LAZY DOG
ZWEI
BOXKÄMPFER
JAGEN
EVA QUER DURCH

BD Console Remix – Italic | Büro Destruct

quick brown

ABCDEFGHIJKLMNOPQ
RSTUVWXYZabcdefg
hijklmnopqrstuvwx
yzäçéöü0123456789!?@

BD Cravt | Büro Destruct

The quick brown מתא

ABCDEFGHIJKLMNOPQRSTUV
WXYZabcdefghijklmnopqrs
tuvwxyzäöü0123456789!?@

BD Dippex | Büro Destruct

The quick brown

ABCDEFGHIJKLMNOPQRSTUVW
XYZabcdefghijklmnopqr
stuvwxy20123456789&!?

BD Eject KTNA – Regular | Büro Destruct

アヂウエオカキクゲコサ
シスセンタヂツテトナニ
ヌネノハヒフォホマミム
ナモヤユヨラリルレボワ

BD Eject KTNA – Lower Phat | Büro Destruct

アヂウエオカキクゲコサ
シスセンタヂツテトナニ
ヌネノハヒフォホマミム
ナモヤユヨラリルレボワ

BD Eject KTNA – Upper Phat | Büro Destruct

アヂウエオカキクゲコサ
シスセンタヂツテトナニ
ヌネノハヒフォホマミム
ナモヤユヨラリルレボワ

243

BD Fimo | Büro Destruct

The quick brown

ABCDEFGHIJKLMNOPQRSTUV
WXYZabcdefghijklmnopqrs
tuvwxyzäçé0123456789&

BD Fimo – Outline | Büro Destruct

The quick brown

ABCDEFGHIJKLMNOPQRSTUV
WXYZabcdefghijklmnopqrs
tuvwxyzäçé0123456789&

BD Flossy | Büro Destruct

BD Gala Quadra — Büro Destruct

quick brown fox jumps

ABCDEFGHIJKLMNOPQRSTUVWX
YZabcdefghijklmnopqrstuvw
xyzããõUБ123456789[&.,!?@]

BD Hexa Des — Büro Destruct

brown fox

ABCDEFGHIJKLMNOPQRST
UVWXYZabcdefghijklmnop
qrstuvwxyz0123456789&

BD Kristallo — Büro Destruct

the quick brown

abcdefghijklmnopqrstu
vwxyzäçéöü0123456789¢

245

THE QUICK BROWN

ABCDEFGHIJKLMNOPQRSTUVW
XYZabcdefghijklmnopqrstu
vwxyzäöü0123456789(&:;!?$)

quick brown
fox jumps over a lazy

abcdefghijklmnopqrstu
vwxyzäçé0123456789&:;!?

BD Sirca RMX | Büro Destruct

Quick brown
Fox jumps over a lazy

abcdefghijklmnopqrstu
vvwxyzäöġéëñ0123456789

BD Spacy 125 | Büro Destruct

Brown Fox

ABCDEFGHIJKLMNOPQRSTU
VWXYZabcdefghijklmnop
qrstuvwxyz0123456789!?

BD Spinner | Büro Destruct

FOX JUMPS OVER
THE QUICK BROWN FOX

ABCDEFGHIJKLMNOPQRSTUV
WXYZ0123456789

247

BD Stereotype	Büro Destruct

QUICK BROWN

ABCDEFGHIJKLMNO
PQRSTUVWXYZÄÇÖ
0123456789(.,/!?$@)

BD Stereotype – Square Up	Büro Destruct

QUICK BROWN

ABCDEFGHIJKLMNO
PQRSTUVWXYZÄÇÖ
0123456789(.,/!?$@)

BD Wakarimasu KTNA	Büro Destruct

イロハニホヘトチリヌル

アイウエオカキクケコサシスセソ
タチツテトナニヌネノハヒフヘホマ
ミムメモヤユヨラリルレロワヲン

Typodermic Fonts

www.typodermic.com
typodermic@gmail.com

QUICK BROWN

ΛΑƷBCDEFGHIJKLMM
NOPPQRSTUVIWWXYZ
0123456789(&:;!?£¥€)

ABCDEFGHIJKLMNOPQRSTUV
WXYZabcdefghijklmnopqrstuv
wxyzążçéġîñøśü0123456789(!?€)

THE QUICK BROWN FOX jumps over a lazy dog. Zwei Boxkämpfer jagen Eva quer durch Sylt. Lorem ipsum dolor sit amet, consectetur adipisicing elit, sed do eiusmod tempor incididunt ut labore et dolore magna aliqua. The quick brown fox jumps over a lazy dog. Zwei

The quick brown

ABCDEFGHIJKLMNOP
QRSTUVWXYZabcdef
ghijklmnopqrstuvwxy
zäçéñO123456789!?

Octin College | Ray Larabie

THE QUICK BROWN FOX

ABCDEFGHIJKLMNOPQRST
UVWXYZĄČĐÉĢŁÑØŘŞŢÜŻ
0123456789(&:;!?$¢£¥€@)

Octin Prison | Ray Larabie

THE QUICK BROWN FOX

ABCDEFGHIJKLMNOPQR
STUVWXYZĄÇÉĢÎÑØŚÜŻ
0123456789(&:;!?$¢£¥€@)

Octin Sports | Ray Larabie

THE QUICK BROWN FOX

ABCDEFGHIJKLMNOPQR
STUVWXYZĄÇÉĢÎÑØŚÜŻ
0123456789(&:;!?$¢£¥€@)

Typodermic Fonts | www.typodermic.com

THE QUICK BROWN FOX JUMPS OVER A LAZY DOG ZWEI BOXKÄMPFER

THE QUICK BROWN FOX

ABCDEFGHIJKLMNOPQRSTU
VWXYZĄČĐÉGÎHŁÑØŘŞŢÜŻ
0123456789(&:;!?$¢£¥€@)

THE QUICK BROWN FOX

ABCDEFGHIJKLMNOPQRST
UVWXYZĄČĐÉGŁÑØŘŞŢÜŻ
0123456789(&:;!?$¢£¥€@)

THE QUICK BROWN FOX

ABCDEFGHIJKLMNOPQR
STUVWXYZĄÇÉGÎÑØSÜŻ
0123456789(&:;!?$¢£¥€@)

ABCDEFGHIJKLMNOPQRSTUVWXY
Zabcdefghijklmnopqrstuvwxyzäçé
0123456789(&:;!?S¢£¥€@)

THE QUICK BROWN FOX jumps over a lazy dog. Zwei Boxkämpfer jagen Eva quer durch Sylt. Lorem ipsum dolor sit amet, consectetur adipisicing elit, sed do eiusmod tempor incididunt ut labore et dolore magna aliqua. The quick brown fox jumps over a lazy dog. Zwei Boxkämpfer jagen Eva quer durch Sylt. Lorem ipsum dolor sit

The quick brown fox

ABCDEFGHIJKLMNOPQ
RSTUVWXYZabcdefghij
klmnopqrstuvwxyzäçéñø
0123456789(&:;!?$€@)

The quick brown fox

ABCDEFGHIJKLMNOPQRST
UVWXYZabcdefghijklmno
pqrstuvwxyz0123456789!?

Vic Fieger

www.vicfieger.com
vic@vicfieger.com

brown fox

abcdefghijklmnopqrs
tuvwxyz0123456789€

BROWN FOX

ABCDEFGHIJKLMNOPQRSTU
VWXYZABCDEFGHIJKLMNOP
QRSTUVWXYZ0123456789!?€

The quick brown fox jumps over

ABCDEFGHIJKLMNOPQRSTUVW
XYZabcdefghijklmnopqrstuvwxyzäçéïñöü
0123456789(&:;!?$€)

Edo | Vic Vieger

BROWN FOX

ABCDEFGHIJKLMNOPQR
STUVWXYZ0123456789€

Eurocentric | Vic Vieger

THE QVICK BROWN

ΛΛBCDEΣFGHIJKLMNΝ
OPQRΛSTVVWXYZÄÇÇ
0123456789

Fawn Script | Vic Vieger

THE QUICK BROWN FOX JUMPS

ABCDEFGHIJKLMNOPQRSTUVWXY
Zabcdefghijklmnopqrstuvwxyzäç
éîñöü0123456789&:;!?$€

LAZY DOG

ABCDEFGHIJKLMNOPQR
STUVWXYZ0123456789

THE QUICK BROWN

ABBCDEFGHIJKLMИN
OPQRSTЦUЏXYZÄ
ÇÉÑÖØ123456789G€

QUICK BROWN
FOX JUMPS OVER

ABCDEFGHIJKLMNOPQR
STUVWXYZ0123456789G

260

THE QUICK
BROWN
FOX JUMPS OVER
A LAZY DOG
ZWEI
BOXKÄMPFER JAGEN

Quick End Jerk | Vic Vieger

THE QUICK BROWN

ABCDEFGHIJKLMNOPQRST
UVWXYZABCDEFGHIJKLMNO
PQRSTUVWXYZ0123456789

Yukarimobile | Vic Vieger

brown fox

abcdefghijklmnopqrs
tuvwxyz0123456789!?

VTKS Design

www.vtks.com.br
vtks@vtks.com.br

VTKS 36 | Douglas Vitkauskas Pereira

QUICK BROWN
THE QUICK BROWN FOX

ABCDEFGHIJKLMNOPQRSTUVWXYZ

VTKS Alcalina | Douglas Vitkauskas Pereira

QUICK BROWN

ABCDEFGHIJKLMNOPQRS
TUVWXYZ0123456789

VTKS Alpes | Douglas Vitkauskas Pereira

THE QUICK BROWN
FOX JUMPS OVER A LAZY DOG

ABCDEFGHIJKLMNOPQRSTUVWXYZ
ABCDEFGHIJKLMNOPQRSTUVWXYZ

VTKS Bandana | Douglas Vitkauskas Pereira

QUICK BROWN

ABCDEFGHIJKLMNOPQRSTUVWX
YZABCDEFGHIJKLMNOPQRSTUVWXYZ

VTKS Beauty | Douglas Vitkauskas Pereira

QUICK BROWN

ABCDEFGHIJKLM
NOPQRSTUVWXYZ

VTKS Blank | Douglas Vitkauskas Pereira

Quick brown

ABCDEFGHIJKLMNOPQRSTUVWXY3a
bcdefghijklmnopqrstuvwxyz0123456789

VTKS Caveirada | Douglas Vitkauskas Pereira

QUICK BROWN
FOX JUMPS OVER A LAZY

ABCDEFGHIJKLMNOPQRS
TUVWXYZO1234567891

VTKS Chip Set | Douglas Vitkauskas Pereira

BROWN FOX

ABCDEFGHIJKLMN
OPQRSTUVWXYZ
ÀÇÉÑÕ@0123456789(&::?)

VTKS Choice | Douglas Vitkauskas Pereira

THE QUICK BROWN FOX JUMPS

ABCDEFGHIJKLMNOPQRSTUVWX
YZÀÃÉÊÍÑÓÔÚÛÝ0123456789!?

VTKS Clean | Douglas Vitkauskas Pereira

THE QUICK BROWN

ABCDEFGHIJKLMNOPQRS
TUVWXYZabcdefghijk
lmnopqrstuvwxyz

VTKS Colagem | Douglas Vitkauskas Pereira

BROWN FOX

ABCDEFGHIJKLM
NOPQRSTUVWXYZ

VTKS Core | Douglas Vitkauskas Pereira

BROWN FOX

ABCDEFGHIJKLMN
OPQRSTUVWXYZ

267

ABCDEFGHIJKLMNOPQR
STUVWXYZ0123456789

ABCDEFGHIJKLMN
OPQRSTUVWXYZ

ABCDEFGHIJKLMNOPQRST
UVWXYZabcdefghijklmnop
qrstuvwxyz0123456789

VTKS Lemon Drop | Douglas Vitkauskas Pereira

BROWN FOX

ABCDEFGHIJKLMN
OPQRSTUVWXYZ

VTKS Mural | Douglas Vitkauskas Pereira

QUICK BROWN FOX

ABCDEFGHIJKLMNOPQR
STUVWXYZabcdefghijklm
nopqrstuvwxyz0123456789

VTKS No Name | Douglas Vitkauskas Pereira

FOX JUMPS OVER

ABCDEFGHIJKLM
NOPQRSTUVWXYZ

VTKS Noba | Douglas Vitkauskas Pereira

the quick brown fox

aBcdefghijklmnopqrs
tuvwxyz0123456789!?

VTKS Quadrada e Gordinha | Douglas Vitkauskas Pereira

BROWN FOX

ABCDEFGHIJKLM
NOPQRSTUVWXY
20123456789!?

VTKS Quadrada e Gordinha 2 | Douglas Vitkauskas Pereira

BROWN FOX

ABCDEFGHIJKLM
NOPQRSTUVWXY
20123456789!?

VTKS Rock Garage Band | Douglas Vitkauskas Pereira

VTKS Rock Garage Band | Douglas Vitkauskas Pereira

THE QUICK BROWN

ABCDEFGHIJKLMN
OPQRSTUVWXYZ

VTKS Scretch | Douglas Vitkauskas Pereira

THE QUICK BROWN

ABCDEFGHIJKLM
NOPQRSTUVXYWZ

VTKS Secret Profile | Douglas Vitkauskas Pereira

QUICK BROWN FOX
JUMPS OVER A LAZY DOG

ABCDEFGHIJKLMNOPQRSTUVWX
YZabcdefghijklmnopqrstuvwxyz0123456789

271

VTKS Sonho | Douglas Vitkauskas Pereira

ABCDEFGHIJKLMNOPQR
STUVWXYZabcdefghijklmno
pqrstuvwxyz0123456789!?@

VTKS Squizita | Douglas Vitkauskas Pereira

THE QUICK BROWN

ABCDEFGHIJKLMNopQRST
UVWXYZÂÇÉÑ0123456789!?

VTKS Stress | Douglas Vitkauskas Pereira

BROWN FOX

ABCDEFGHIJKLMNOPQRST
UVWXYZabcdefghijklmnopqrstuvwxyz0123456789

The quick brown fox jumps over a LAZY dog Lorem ipsum dolor

Quick brown fox jumps over

ABCDEFGHIJKLMNOPQRSTUV
WXYZabcdefghijklmnopqrstuvwxyz

QUICK BROWN
FOX JUMPS OVER A LAZY

ABCDEFGhiJKLMNOPQRST
UVWXYZäçÉÑ0123456789

QUICK BROWN

ABCDEFGHIJKLMNOPQRS
TUVWXYZ0123456789!?

WC Fonts

www.wcfonts.com
christopheferay@wanadoo.fr

The quick brown

ABCDEFGHIJKLMNOPQRSTU
VWXYZabcdefghijklmnopqrs
tuvwxyzäçé0123456789(&:;!?)

The quick brown

ABCDEFGHIJKLMNOPQRS
TUVWXYZabcdefghijklmno
pqrstuvwxyz0123456789&!?

BROWN FOX

ABCDEFGHIJKLMNOPQRSTU
VWXYZabcdefghijklmnop
qrstuvwxyz0123456789

The quick brown fox jumps over

ABCDEFGHIJKLMNOPQRSTUVWX
YZabcdefghijklmnopqrstuvwxyz
äçéñö0123456789(&!?$£¥€@)

The quick brown fox jumps over

ABCDEFGHIJKLMNOPQRSTUVWX
YZabcdefghijklmnopqrstuvwxyz
äçéñö0123456789(&!?$£¥€@)

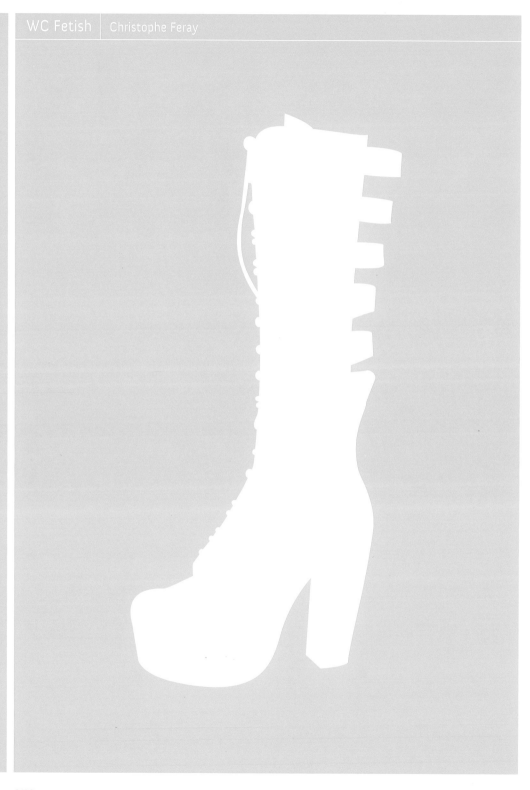

WC Roughtrad   Christophe Feray

The quick brown

ABCDEFGHIJKLMNOPQRST
UVWXYZabcdefghijklmnopqr
stuvwxyzäçé0123456789&!?

Quick brown

ABCDEFGHI/KLMNOPQRSTU
VWWXYZabcdefghijklmnopqrstu
vwxyzäçéñø0123456789(&!?€)

The quick brown fox

ABCDEFGHIJKLMNOPQRSTU
VWXYZabcdefghijklmnopqrst
uvwxyzäёñ0123456789(&!?)

The quick brown fox

ABCDEFGHIJKLMNOPQRSTU
VWXYZabcdefghijklmnopqrst
uvwxyzäёñ0123456789(&!?)

The quick brown fox

ABCDEFGHIJKLMNOPQRSTU
VWXYZabcdefghijklmnopqrst
uvwxyzäéñ0123456789(&!?)

The quick brown fox

ABCDEFGHIJKLMNOPQRSTU
VWXYZabcdefghijklmnopqrst
uvwxyzäéñ0123456789(&!?)

ABCDEFGHIJKLMNOPQRSTUVWXYZabcd
efghijklmnopqrstuvwxyzäçéîñöøüœ
0123456789(&et¿:;!?$¢¥€@)

THE QUICK BROWN FOX jumps over a lazy dog. Zwei Boxkämpfer jagen Eva quer durch Sylt. Lorem ipsum dolor sit amet, consectetur adipisicing elit, sed do eiusmod tempor incididunt ut labore et dolore magna aliqua. The quick brown fox jumps over a lazy dog. Zwei Boxkämpfer jagen Eva quer durch Sylt. Lorem ipsum dolor

ABCDEFGHIJKLMNOPQRSTUVWXYZabcd
efghijklmnopqrstuvwxyzäçéîñöøüœß
0123456789(&et¿:;!?$¢¥€@)

THE QUICK BROWN FOX jumps over a lazy dog. Zwei Boxkämpfer jagen Eva quer durch Sylt. Lorem ipsum dolor sit amet, consectetur adipisicing elit, sed do eiusmod tempor incididunt ut labore et dolore magna aliqua. The quick brown fox jumps over a lazy dog. Zwei Boxkämpfer jagen Eva quer durch Sylt. Lorem ipsum dolor sit amet,

ABCDEFGHIJKLMNOPQRSTUVWXYZabcdef
ghijklmnopqrstuvwxyzäçéîñöøšüžæœß
0123456789(&et¿:;!?$¢¥€@)

THE QUICK BROWN FOX jumps over a lazy dog. Zwei Boxkämpfer jagen Eva quer durch Sylt. Lorem ipsum dolor sit amet, consectetur adipisicing elit, sed do eiusmod tempor incididunt ut labore et dolore magna aliqua. The quick brown fox jumps over a lazy dog. Zwei Boxkämpfer jagen Eva quer durch Sylt. Lorem ipsum dolor sit amet, consec-

Kaffeesatz – Bold | Jan Gerner

ABCDEFGHIJKLMNOPQRSTUVWXYZabcdefg
hijklmnopqrstuvwxyzäåçéëïñøšûüžæœß
0123456789(&℮t₵:;!?$¢¥€@)

THE QUICK BROWN FOX jumps over a lazy dog. Zwei Boxkämpfer jagen Eva quer durch Sylt. Lorem ipsum dolor sit amet, consectetur adipisicing elit, sed do eiusmod tempor incididunt ut labore et dolore magna aliqua. The quick brown fox jumps over a lazy dog. Zwei Boxkämpfer jagen Eva quer durch Sylt. Lorem ipsum dolor sit amet, consectetur adipisicing

Tagesschrift | Jan Gerner

The quick brown fox

ABCDEFGHIJKLMNOPQRST
UVWXYZabcdefghijklmnopq
rstuvwxyz0123456789(&!?€)

Interviews (DE)

Jos Buivenga – exljbris

Jos Buivenga hat sich in den letzten Jahren einen Namen als neues Talent in der Welt der Schriftgestaltung gemacht. Am Anfang waren viele Leute nur sprachlos über die wunderschönen kostenlosen Fonts, die er erschaffen hatte. Nun hat er seine erste kommerzielle Schriftart, Museo, erstellt, die zurzeit die Bestsellerliste von MyFonts anführt. Als ich mich entschieden hatte, in diesem Buch die Schriftart Anivers zu verwenden, hat Jos großzügig angeboten, Anivers in kursiv und fett zu erstellen, um die typografische Palette zu vergrößern. Es ist jetzt an der Zeit, diesen Niederländer etwas besser kennen zu lernen.

Ihre Fonts werden zu den besten kostenlosen Schriften gezählt, die zurzeit verfügbar sind. Diese sind so gut wie viele kommerzielle Schriftarten, die verfügbar sind, und beinhalten die gleichen umfassenden Zeichensätze. Warum geben Sie diese kostenlos weg?

JB: Ich hatte mir keinen festen Plan gemacht, als ich meine erste Schriftart, Delicious, erstellt hatte. Ich war einfach von der Idee fasziniert, einen Text mit meiner eigenen Schriftart zu setzen. Da ich kein Fontdesign studiert hatte, lag die Herausforderung in der Entdeckung aller Probleme und dem Finden geeigneter Lösungen, um meine eigene Schrift mit einem passablen Äußeren zu erstellen. Delicious. Der Gedanke an einen Verkauf des Fonts kam nie auf … es war einfach ein tolles Erlebnis, dass der Font den Leuten gefallen hat oder sie die Schrift verwenden wollten. Ich hatte mich erst nach zehn Jahren entschieden, eine neue Schrift zu erstellen. Fontin fühlte sich immer noch wie eine typographische Entdeckungsreise an, die ich lieber mit Leuten teilen wollte als diese zu verkaufen. Kurz nachdem ich Fontin abgeschlossen hatte, wurden meine Schriften in der Liste „25 Best Free Quality Fonts" (Die 25 besten kostenlosen Qualitätsfonts)

von Vitaly Friedman aufgeführt und dann ging es richtig los. Viele Leute lernten mich und meine kostenlosen Schriften kennen und ihre Reaktionen waren bewegend – so sehr, dass ich mich entschlossen habe, jede Schrift, die ich machen würde, kostenlos zur Verfügung zu stellen.

Mit Museo und der neuen Version Ihrer Anivers Schriftart haben Sie sich entschieden, ein neues Verfahren zu verwenden. Einige der Schriftgewichte werden als ein kostenloser Download zur Verfügung gestellt und die anderen Schriftgewichte sind gegen eine geringe Bezahlung erhältlich. Was führte zu dieser Änderung?

JB: Ich hatte etwa 12 Jahren lang fünf Tage die Woche gearbeitet. Ich wollte mehr Zeit für das Entwerfen von Schriften haben und als ich die Möglichkeit bekam, die Stelle zu wechseln und einen Tag weniger die Woche zu arbeiten, war ich sehr froh darüber. Ich wollte gerne kostenpflichtige Fonts anbieten, sodass ich eine bestimmte finanzielle Kompensierung für diesen Tag erhalten könnte.

Könnten Sie den Prozess beschreiben, dem Sie folgen, wenn Sie eine Schriftart entwerfen?

JB: Ich mache viele Skizzen. Ich kann die meisten Skizzen nicht verwenden, aber dies macht nichts aus, ich tue es sehr gerne. Ich verwende oft diese Entwürfe als einen Ausgangspunkt für eine neue Schriftart, aber der echte Prozess findet auf dem Bildschirm statt. Ich beginne immer mit einigen Kleinbuchstaben (a, c, e, f, g, h, i, n, s und v) damit ich ein Gefühl für die neue Schriftart bekomme. Wenn mir diese gefallen, erstelle ich den restlichen Teil der Kleinbuchstaben und dabei oftmals auch die Großbuchstaben H und O, damit ich einen Gesamteindruck erhalten kann, wie alles zusammenpasst. Wenn ich ebenfalls geplant habe, fette und kursive Buchstaben zu erstellen, mache ich einige Grobentwürfe, damit ich sehen kann, ob die normale Schrift angepasst werden muss, damit alle Schriftgewichte und Stile funktionieren. Im

Normalfall stecke ich die Vor- und Nachbreite grob ab während ich an jeder Glyphe arbeite und führe eine Reihe von Ausrichtungen aus, bis der Abstand stimmt. Es ist dann an der Zeit, die Zeichen zu unterschneiden und die Schriftart in unterschiedlichen Situationen zu testen. Nachdem dies alles abgeschlossen ist, generiere ich ein Final Beta für das Kompatibilitätstesten auf verschiedenen Plattformen und mit unterschiedlichen Anwendungen. Wenn alles so ist wie es sein sollte, kann ich letztendlich die neue Schriftart veröffentlichen.

Was sind Ihre Zukunftspläne?

JB: Ich arbeite zurzeit an Museo Sans als Begleitung für Museo. Darauf folgt Calluna, mein erster seriöser Versuch, eine Buchschrift zu erstellen. Nicht zuletzt: DeliciousX und Fontin Serif warten darauf, noch abgeschlossen zu werden und ich muss Fontin (Semi) und Fontin Sans für erweiterte Sprachunterstützung aktualisieren. Oftmals bekomme ich eine neue Idee (wie z.B. Calluna während ich an Museo gearbeitet habe) und dann mache ich eine „Pause", um zu untersuchen, ob sich die Arbeit lohnen würde. Es passiert immer auf eine sehr natürliche Art und Weise und ich muss mir nie Gedanken machen, was ich als nächstes tun werde. Manchmal wünsche ich mir ich könnte mich in drei Teile teilen, damit ich alle Ideen realisieren könnte, die ich habe.

Janusz Marian Nowacki

Ich habe lange nach einer digitalen Version meiner polnischen Lieblingsschrift aus Metalllettern, dem Antykwa Półtawskiego, gesucht. Ich habe mich erkundigt und entdeckte dabei die Organisation GUST (die polnische Benutzergruppe für die kostenlose Schriftsatzsoftware TeX), die diese Schrift kostenlos auf ihrer Website angeboten hat. Die Qualität war sehr gut

und auf der gleichen Website fand ich eine Reihe von anderen, äußerst sorgfältig gestalteten, wiederbelebten Versionen polnischer Metallletter-Schriftarten. Diese hatten alle eines gemein: Janusz Marian Nowacki.

Wie haben Sie die Idee bekommen, klassische polnische Schriftarten zu digitalisieren?

JMN: Der erste Rechner erschien 1990 auf meinem Schreibtisch – zur gleichen Zeit wie die Änderung des politischen Systems in Polen. Ich war damals 40 und damit begann mein Abenteuer mit Computern. Bis zu dem Zeitpunkt wusste ich noch nichts davon. Ich musste alles von der Pieke auf lernen. Ich bin Journalist von Beruf. Ich verbrachte früher viel Zeit in einer Druckerei und habe den Schriftsatz der Zeitung, bei der ich tätig war, beaufsichtigt, bis 1981 der Ausnahmezustand ausgerufen wurde. Zu der Zeit habe ich mich mit den Grundlagen der Typografie bekannt gemacht und lernte erfahrene Schriftsetzer kennen. Ich habe mich ebenfalls mit polnischen Metallschriftarten bekannt gemacht. Als ich zum Rechner wechselte war ich von den typografischen Möglichkeiten, die verfügbar waren, enttäuscht. Rechnerunterstützte Typografie schien weniger kompliziert und bot neue Möglichkeiten. Ich konnte jedoch nicht meine polnischen Lieblingsschriftarten verwenden. Die einzigen Schriftarten, die verfügbar waren, waren Times, Helvetica und Courier. Wenn man etwas anderes wollte, gab es zwei Möglichkeiten: die Schriftart entweder kaufen oder selbst erstellen. Da ich keine polnischen Schriftarten kaufen konnte, habe ich mich für letzteres entschieden.

Können Sie mir sagen wie Sie mit dem Entwurf von Schriftarten begonnen haben?

JMN: Meine ersten Versuche beim Entwurf von Schriftarten waren so primitiv und unerfolgreich, dass ich diese besser nicht erwähnen sollte. Ich begann 1994 seriös an der ersten Version von Antykwa Toruńska zu arbeiten. Die Zeichnungen der

289

einzelnen Buchstaben wurden in CorelDraw erstellt und wurden daraufhin in Fontographer importiert. Die Ergebnisse waren zwar akzeptabel, aber später stellte sich heraus, dass sie noch einiges zu wünschen übrig ließen. Schriftarten sind nicht nur schöne Buchstabenformen, sondern enthalten auch eine ganze Reihe von technischen Problemen, mit denen sich ein Designer nicht befassen muss.

Welches Material haben Sie für die Digitalisierung verwendet? Ich weiß, dass Sie für die Schriftart Antykwa Toruńska Zugang zu den ursprünglichen Entwürfen hatten.
JMN: Die Quelle für die erste Version war ein Katalog der Warszawska Odlewnia Czcionek (Warschauer Schriftenherausgeber). Nachdem ich einen Entwurf von Antykwa Toruńska vorbereitet hatte, habe ich dem Schöpfer der Schriftart, Zygfryd Gardzielewski, mit einem riesigen Stapel von Ausdrucken einen Besuch abgestattet. Wir haben jeden Buchstaben gründlich besprochen und ich habe meine Ideen angepasst. Zygfryd Gardzielewski akzeptierte die Idee, Schriften zu produzieren. Er wusste, dies wäre die einzige Art und Weise seine Arbeit zu bewahren, da die Änderungen in der Drucktechnologie zur Folge hatten, dass nur Formate, die im Computer eingelesen werden können, überleben würden. Als ein Abschiedsgeschenk gab er mir die Entwurfsmaterialien, die er noch hatte. So musste ich zwar erneut beginnen, aber dieses Mal hatte ich eine bessere Quelle von Schriftmaterialien. Ich habe Zygfryd Gardzielewski bis zu seinem Tode 2001 als technischen Berater gehabt. Danach musste ich meine Entwurfsprobleme alleine lösen.

Sie haben sich entschieden, die Menge von Glyphen für die Schriftarten weit über die ursprüngliche Anzahl von Sprachen, die unterstützt wurden, zu erweitern...
JMN: Die ursprünglichen Schriftarten von Antykwa Toruńska erlaubten nur das Setzen von Text in ein

paar Sprachen mit lateinischem Alphabet: Polnisch, Deutsch, Französisch und Englisch. In Polen wurden 1950, der Zeit der Erstellung dieser Schriften, keine andere Sprachen benötigt. In der ersten veröffentlichten Version habe ich einige akzentuierte Buchstaben und unterschiedliche Zeichen hinzugefügt, die für den Computer-Schriftsatz benötigt werden und nicht im Metallschriftsatz aufgeführt sind. Das Grundformat für die Schriften war Post-Script Type1, in dem nur 256 Zeichen möglich sind. Nach der Einführung des neuen OpenType Formats wurde es mir möglich, mehr mit der Schriftart zu machen und ich begann mit dem Entwerfen von Zeichen, mit denen sich Zygfryd Gardzielewski nicht befasst hatte. Ich erstellte griechische und kyrillische Buchstaben, mathematische Symbole und einen Satz mit lateinischen Buchstaben, die es möglich machen, Texte in äußerst exotischen Sprachen zu setzen, wie beispielsweise Vietnamesisch oder Navajo. Natürlich war es überhaupt nicht so einfach, ich bin schließlich kein professioneller Designer. Die Benutzer müssen meine Arbeit bewerten.

Wenn man die unglaubliche Zeitinvestition in Anbetracht zieht, die für solche Projekte notwendig ist, was war der ausschlaggebende Grund, dass Sie sich entschieden haben die Schriften kostenlos verfügbar zu machen?
JMN: Wäre ich mir von Anfang an bewusst gewesen, wie schwierig es ist, Schriften zu erstellen und welche technologischen Probleme ich zu bewältigen hätte, wäre ich wahrscheinlich gar nicht damit begonnen. Es ist mir jedoch gelungen, die Probleme zu lösen, die auftraten und dies ist äußerst befriedigend gewesen. Ich habe mich hauptsächlich mit Schriften beschäftigt, die von Polen entworfen sind. Wir scheinen als eine Nation kein Talent zu haben, uns selbst ins Rampenlicht zu stellen und dies macht es für uns schwierig, unsere Produkte auf den Weltmarkt zu bringen. Aus diesem Grund habe ich mich entschieden, für die Fonts kein Geld

zu verlangen. Auf diese Weise könnten sie beliebter werden. Ich bin der Meinung, dass polnische Schriftarten zum weltweiten Kulturerbe gehören und möchte, dass jeder diese verwenden kann, der daran interessiert ist.

FontStruct

Anfang 2008 wurde ein neues Programm für die Bearbeitung von Fonts in Form einer Website vorgestellt. FontStruct, der Name dieser raffinierten Software, hat die Schriftsatz- und Designgemeinde im Sturm erobert. Sie kann gratis benutzt werden und die Macher der Website ermutigen die Benutzer, die Schriften, die sie erstellt haben, anderen zur Verfügung zu stellen. Ich musste einfach mehr erfahren und habe deshalb mit Rob Meek, dem Gründer des ganzen, und Stephen Coles, seinem Sponsor und auch Schriftdirektor von FontShop International, ein Gespräch geführt.

Woher stammt die ursprüngliche Idee für das FontStruct Programm?
RM: FontStruct hat sich aus einer langjährigen Faszination mit modularen Fonts heraus entwickelt. Modulare Schriften machen Spaß und sind relativ einfach zu machen; sie sind ideal für jemanden, der Interesse daran hat, mit Systemen und innerhalb von Grenzen zu spielen. Und ich glaube sie sind ebenfalls ein guter Ausgangspunkt für jemanden, der an typografischem Entwurf interessiert ist. FontStruct wurde als ein Werkzeug für die Entwicklung solcher Fonts erschaffen. Es wurde so gestaltet, dass es einfach und nicht technisch ist. Es hat ebenfalls einiges gemeinsam mit meinen MEEK Typographic Synthesizern (typografische Synthesizer) – einer Reihe von zugänglichen Spielzeugen für das Entwerfen von Fonts. Die MEEK Typographic Synthesizer sind unterhaltsame, esoterische

Übungen. Mit FontStruct wollte ich versuchen etwas zu entwickeln, das für eine breitere Gruppe von Nutzen und Interesse wäre.

Wie kam es zur Beteiligung von FontShop in der Entwicklung von FontStruct?
SC: FontShop und Rob Meek haben schon seit geraumer Zeit ein enges Arbeitsverhältnis, wobei eine Reihe von Verbesserungen an FontShop.com hinzugefügt worden sind. Rob hat uns in Bezug auf das FontStruct Konzept angesprochen und uns gebeten, als Sponsor zu agieren und bei der Produktion der Website mit zu wirken.

War es Ihre ursprüngliche Idee diese Software als eine Website verfügbar zu machen?
RM: Ja. Ich finde, dass Schriften sich äußerst gut für die neue Ära von Onlinekreation und zum Teilen eignen. Die relativ kleinen Dateigrößen und der klar gegliederte schöpferische Raum eignen sich gerade für das Browser-basierte Bearbeiten. Ich hoffe, dass FontStruct sich zu einer Art von Mini-Flickr/Picnic für die Welt der modularen Fonts entwickelt.

Worin sehen Sie den zu Grunde liegenden Zweck von FontStruct?
SC: Es gibt keine bessere Art und Weise Anerkennung für die Schriften und die Fertigkeiten, die für den Entwurf benötigt werden, zu bekommen als selbst einmal einen Versuch in diesem Handwerk zu unternehmen. Aus diesem Grund ist das Zeichnen von Buchstaben auch oftmals ein Teil von Typografie- und Grafikdesignkursen an Hochschulen. FontStruct ist Teil der Aufgabe von FontShop, das allgemeine Bewusstsein für Schriften zu erhöhen und den wahrgenommenen Wert von gut gemachten digitalen Schriftarten zu steigern. Das Erzeugen und Teilen von Schrift ist eine ausgezeichnete Art dieses Ziel zu erreichen und der kostenlose Zugang ist essenziell, um eine offene und blühende Gemeinde zu erschaffen.
RM: Persönlich hoffe ich, dass es Anfängern eine

unterhaltsame Einführung in die Freuden der typografischen Erschaffung ermöglicht und für erfahrenere Schüler zu einem Spielplatz der modularen Fonts wird.

Schaffen Sie sich nicht selbst Konkurrenz für die modularen Schriftarten, die Sie selbst verkaufen, indem Sie Benutzer von FontStruct dazu ermutigen, ihre Fonts kostenlos verfügbar zu machen?
SC: Der FontStructor (der Editor innerhalb von FontStruct) ermöglicht dem Benutzer einen erstaunlichen Grad an Flexibilität, wie die Fonts zeigen, die sich zurzeit in unserer Sammlung befinden. In diesem Sinne könnte es für einen Schrifthändler als ein Wagnis gesehen werden, kostenlose Downloads zu erlauben. Jedoch erlauben die Beschränkungen des Rasters nicht die Erstellung von Schriftarten auf professionellem Niveau. Letztendlich fördern wir mit FontStruct eine weltweite Gemeinde von Schriftenthusiasten, was für FontShop und die gesamte Industrie nur von Vorteil sein kann.

Rob, Sie haben eine Reihe von Schriften mit FontStruct erstellt, die in diesem Buch aufgeführt werden. Liegt Ihre Leidenschaft im Entwerfen von Fonts oder eher in der Kreieren von Werkzeugen, die andere beim Entwerfen unterstützen?
RM: Ohne Frage das letztere. Der Umstand, dass ich sowohl als Entwerfer als auch typografischer Amateur und ferner noch als Softwareentwickler Erfahrung gesammelt habe war zweifellos für das Projekt von Vorteil. Ich habe große Ehrfurcht vor Leuten mit wahrer typografischer Leidenschaft. Wenn ich die erstaunlichen Dinge sehe, die andere mit dem Tool gemacht haben, ist dies eine große Ehre für mich.

Probieren Sie es selbst:
fontstruct.fontshop.com

Brode Vosloo

Brode Vosloo erreichte allgemeine Bekanntheit aufgrund seiner Fonts, die versuchen, den wahren afrikanischen Geist einzufangen. Sie haben nichts mit den stereotypischen Fonts gemein, die von Tourismusorganisationen eingesetzt werden, um diesen Kontinent zu repräsentieren. Seine Inspiration nimmt er direkt von den Schriften, die er in den Straßen Afrikas findet. Seine Schriftherausgeberei mit dem Namen „The Sacred Nipple", die inzwischen nicht mehr existiert, genoß viel Aufmerksamkeit. Vosloo produzierte sogar eine Reihe von Schriften für den amerikanischen Kultherausgeber T.26 von Carlos Segura. Und dann wurde es still um ihn.

Die meisten Ihrer Fonts wurden als kostenlose Schriften veröffentlicht. Warum haben Sie sich entschieden, diesen Weg einzuschlagen, anstatt Geld für die Schriften zu verlangen?
BV: Obwohl ich an einer der renommiertesten Designschulen in Südafrika Grafikdesign studiert habe, hatte ich nicht die Möglichkeit, mit erfahrenen Schriftsetzern oder Meistern von Fontsoftware wie z.B. Fontographer zu arbeiten. Ich musste mir eigentlich alles selbst über die Typografie und die Software beibringen, die für die Herstellung funktioneller Fonts verwendet wird. Die ersten Fonts waren experimentelle Versuche in der Welt der Typografie und ich war ehrlich gesagt nicht der Meinung, dass ich dafür Geld verlangen könnte. Während ich meine typografische Reise fortführte, erkannte ich die Notwendigkeit von Schriften, die eine afrikanischere Natur hatten – Schriften, die das Erdige und die Energie des afrikanischen Lebens wiedergeben. Fonts die sich von den kitschigen Touristenschriften abheben, die in der Zeit verwendet wurden, um Afrika zu repräsentieren. Und auf diese Art wurden kostenlose Fonts wie beispielsweise iAlfabhethi, iZulu, Mr CV Joint, Pleine Str.,

Rural und Star Salon geschaffen. Unter der Führung von Carlos Segura habe ich dann anschließend vollständig funktionelle kostenpflichtige Fonts erstellt, die komplette Zeichensätze aufwiesen wie z.B. die Shoe Repairs und Freeline Sammlungen und den Pi-Font Afrodisiac. Diese Schriften werden zurzeit über die T.26 Schriftherausgeberei von Segura veröffentlicht.

Warum haben Sie aufgehört kostenlose Fonts zu erstellen?

BV: In den späten Neunzigern schien es als ob jeder mit einem Rechner und irgendeiner Software zur Fonterstellung Schriftsetzer wurde. Es gab – und dies wird bestimmt immer noch der Fall sein – zahlreiche kostenlose Schriften. Jedoch sind diese Fonts oftmals nur Neuinterpretationen von Schriften, die von anderen Entwerfern Mitte der Neunziger geschaffen wurden. Ich begann den Eindruck zu bekommen, dass alles, was über das Internet kostenlos weggegeben wurde, keinen Wert hatte. Nachdem ich meinen Shoe Repairs Font veröffentlicht hatte, waren mir aus erster Hand die Mühen und Freuden bewusst geworden, die mit der anstrengenden Aufgabe, eine vollständige und funktionelle Schrift zu erstellen, einhergehen. Ich war vom Umstand betrübt, dass Menschen kostenlosen Schriften den Vorzug gaben gegenüber Schriften, die von erfahrenen Schriftsetzern geschaffen wurden. Sogar die einfachste Schrift benötigt einen gewissen Grad von Voraussicht und Einsatz, zwei Aspekte des Fontdesigns, wobei ich der Meinung bin, dass diese eine gewisse finanzielle Belohnung wert sind. Verstehen Sie mich jedoch bitte nicht falsch, ich habe keine negative Einstellung zum Veröffentlichen von kostenlosen Fonts. Ich glaube, dass der Computer die Möglichkeit der Erstellung von Schriften in die Hände des gewöhnlichen Designers gelegt hat und es damit möglich gemacht hat, eine Reihe von phantastischen Ideen umzusetzen. Kostenlose Fonts haben mit Sicherheit neues Leben in ein Handwerk gehaucht, das

zuvor einer auserlesenen Elite vorbehalten war. Ich denke, gute Fonts sind wie alle anderen guten Produkte, das beste bewährt sich immer.

Es ist eine lange Zeit her, seit Sie Ihre letzte Schrift erstellt haben. Haben Sie sich in Ihrer Arbeit auf etwas anderes gerichtet?

BV: Es ist wirklich eine ganze Zeit her, seit ich meine letzte Schrift veröffentlicht habe. Dies liegt hauptsächlich an dem Umstand, dass ich mich von einem Arbeitsumfeld, das ausschließlich auf Grafikdesign gerichtet war, in andere Bereiche wie Bewegungs- und Modedesign bewegt habe. Ich habe mir immer noch Ideen für neue Fonts notiert und habe diese auch in meiner Arbeit verwendet. Ich arbeite jetzt in der Extremsportindustrie für einen Hersteller, dessen Ursprung im Motocross liegt und der nun seine Position im Lifestyle von BMX, Surfing und Wakeboarding gefestigt hat. Ich bin der Marketingmanager des Betriebes und meine Tätigkeit ist die ideale Mischung zwischen meinen Design- und Kommunikationsfähigkeiten und meiner aktiven Teilnahme am Extremsport. Die meisten meiner Ideen für neue Schriften, an denen ich zurzeit arbeite, sind diesem Lebensstil entliehen. Fonts, die verwegen und modisch sind und der Länge eines Fahrradrahmens oder der Kante eines Surfbretts entlang verlaufen können, aus Vinyl geschnitten, bestickt oder geätzt; Schriften, die von Tätowierungen oder Hautritzungen inspiriert sind und einfach dupliziert werden können; Fonts, die sich gut auf Bildschirme übertragen lassen und einfach animiert werden können und dabei ihre Lesbarkeit bewahren. Obwohl meine Ideen für neue Schriften von zahlreichen Quellen stammen, glaube ich, dass die Idee mindestens eines meiner vier Kriterien erfüllen muss, damit sie die Mühe wert ist, in einen vollständig funktionellen Font umgesetzt zu werden. Die Kriterien sind wie folgt: es muss zeitlos, konzeptuell, funktionell oder strukturell sein. Ich bin sicher, dass ich noch einmal Zeit haben werde, einige neue Schriften zu veröffentlichen, aber bis dann werde ich hart arbeiten und daneben nach Herzenslust meine Geländemaschine fahren und surfen. Ich denke, wenn eine Schrift gut ist, macht es nichts aus, ob diese jetzt oder erst in zehn Jahren veröffentlich wird. In der Zwischenzeit werde ich neue Ideen notieren und diese Jahre verwenden, die Spreu vom Weizen zu trennen und die tollen Fonts zu genießen, die es zurzeit gibt.

Lopetz – Büro Destruct

Büro Destruct steht seit Mitte der neunziger Jahre an der Spitze des modernen schweizerischen Grafikdesigns. Ihre Arbeit hat dank zwei Büchern, die im Die Gestalten Verlag erschienen sind, Designer weltweit beeinflusst. Von Anfang an haben sie Schriften entworfen, die zu ihrem originellen Stil passen und sie haben sich entschieden, einen beträchtlichen Teil dieser Fonts anderen Entwerfern zur Verfügung zu stellen, und zwar kostenlos.

Als Sie damit begannen, die ersten Fonts des Büro Destruct für die Verwendung in Ihrer eigenen Arbeit zu erstellen, haben Sie diese sofort für die öffentliche Verwendung freigegeben, etwas das Sie heute immer noch tun?
L: Schriftendesign hat immer eine wichtige Rolle in unserer Arbeit eingenommen. Der Hauptgrund, originelle, maßgeschneiderte Schriftarten zu erstellen war es, eine einzigartige Sprache in unserem täglichen Grafikdesign zu sprechen. Der zweite Grund ist es, die Fonts, die daraus resultieren, zu veröffentlichen und auf diese Art mit unseren Schriftdesigner und anderen Designern zu teilen.

Wie entscheiden Sie welche Schriften Sie kostenlos und welche Sie kostenpflichtig veröffentlichen?
L: Es hängt von der Menge Arbeit ab, die mit der Erstellung einer Schriftart einhergeht. Im Allge-

meinen sind kostenlose Fonts Schriften, die in der Erstellung nicht allzu zeitaufwendig sind. Je professioneller wir eine Schrift machen (Arbeit in Bezug auf Unterschneiden, unterschiedliche Stile, Lesbarkeit), desto größer ist die Chance, dass dies ein kostenpflichtiger Font sein wird. Es wird am Ende immer abgewogen wie nützlich ein Font ist. Wenn wir der Meinung sind, dass die Schrift für einen Werbespot oder eine Anzeige für eine große Firma mit einem großen Budget verwendet werden kann, dann befinden wir uns im kostenpflichtigen Fontbereich.

Sie sind ein renommiertes Grafikdesignstudio. Sind Sie der Meinung, dass dies bei der Akzeptanz ihrer Schriften durch andere Designer hilft?
L: Sicherlich kommt unser Status den kostenlosen und ebenfalls den kostenpflichtigen Fonts zu gute. Aber wir sehen dies von einer anderen Perspektive: Unsere Fonts helfen uns dabei, ein „renommiertes Grafikdesignstudio" zu werden. Im Vergleich zu anderen Schriftdesigner werden unsere Fonts als weniger seriös eingestuft, aber das liegt an der Art wie wir an diesen arbeiten. Wir sehen es mehr als das Spielen auf einem experimentellen Tummelplatz anstatt des seriösen, harten und präzisen Arbeitens. Es war nicht unser Ziel, ein neues Helvetica, Garamond oder etwas vergleichbares zu erschaffen – dafür wären Jahre notwendig, um dies zu bewerkstelligen. Wir möchten neue Grafikformen kreieren, die in einem Alphabet gesammelt und dann verfügbar gemacht werden können. Dies ist noch die gleiche Art auf die wir in den Anfangsjahren von Büro Destruct 1995 mit dem Erstellen von Fonts begonnen haben. Beispielsweise war der flossy Font, unsere erste Fontarbeit, einfach eine Sammlung einer Schafsfigur in unterschiedlichen Posen.

Könnten Sie den Prozess beschreiben, dem Sie folgen, wenn Sie Ihre Fonts entwerfen? Haben Sie zuerst eine Idee für eine Schrift oder haben Sie eine Idee für ein Designprojekt, wobei Sie der Meinung

sind, dass Sie dafür eine neue Schriftart benötigen?
L: Normalerweise wird ein neuer Font des Büro Destruct ins Leben gerufen, nachdem ein Markenzeichen, ein Titel auf einem Konzertposter bzw. Flyer oder einer CD-Hülle erstellt wurde. Das beste Beispiel ist der Font BD Balduin, der ursprünglich das Logo für den Musikinterpreten Balduin war. Manchmal wird eine Schrift durch eine einfache Form erzeugt, die wir in einem ganzen Alphabet ausprobieren möchten. Eine tolle Inspirationsquelle ist das Reisen in andere Länder, die andere Sprachen bzw. nicht-lateinische Alphabete wie z.B. japanische Zeichen oder arabische Buchstaben verwenden. Wir können diese nicht lesen – wir schauen nur auf die Formen und verwenden sie wiederum in unseren Alphabeten.

Verwenden Sie häufig erneut die Fonts, die Sie bereits haben, für Ihre Designarbeit?
L: Unsere Richtlinie ist es diese zu verwenden, wenn es Sinn macht, da sie unsere originelle Sprache sprechen, aber häufiger benutzen wir andere Fonts. Ein wichtiger Grund dafür ist, dass wir Schriften erstellen, die immer mit einem bestimmten Projekt oder einer bestimmten Quelle in Verbindung gebracht werden. Diese gehören dann zu dem betreffenden Projekt bzw. zu einer bestimmten Periode. Die neuen Schriften, die wir machen, teilen wir mit anderen Entwerfern und es ist für uns eine größere Überraschung zu sehen wie andere Designer diese in ihren eigenen Kontext setzen.

Shamrock

Shamrock (auch bekannt als Jeroen Klaver). Er ist vor allem für seine wunderschönen Illustrationen bekannt, die ein Retro-Gefühl haben. Wenige wissen, dass er tatsächlich einen Grad in Grafikdesign hat und sowohl kostenlose als auch kostenpflichtige Fonts erstellt. Viele

seiner Schriftarten spiegeln die Atmosphäre seines Zeichenstils wieder, indem er die meisten passend zu seinen eigenen Illustrationen erstellt. Verwendet man seine Fonts, sitzt in dem Endergebnis dann ein Teil seines künstlerischen Geistes – die Schriften sind witzig, animiert und unwiderstehlich.

Ich war mit Ihren Illustrationen bekannt, aber weniger mit Ihren Schriften. Welchen Platz nehmen Ihre Schriftarten in Ihrer Arbeit ein?
S: Einen sehr wichtigen Platz. Ich begann als Grafikdesigner, da ich immer sehr gerne Sachen wie Zines und Flyer machte. Ich bin nicht die Art von Designer, der ein Bild bestellt, etwas Text darüber klebt und es abliefert. Ich möchte ein Gesamtwerk machen. Alles muss gut gemacht sein und es muss in Balance sein. Ich achte dabei auch sehr auf den Text. Ich habe schon Aufträge abgelehnt, weil das Geschriebene überhaupt keinen Sinn gemacht hat. Wenn man alles selbst macht, kann man das machen wie man will! Ich bin auch immer daran interessiert wie Dinge gemacht werden. Ich weiß, dass es immer Leute gibt, die Sachen viel besser können als ich; aber da ich Dinge auch selbst ausprobiere, bekomme ich einen unglaublichen Respekt für diese Leute und es vereinfacht die Kommunikation mit ihnen.
Ich begann seriös mit dem Zeichnen von Buchstaben in der Schule. Ich verbringe viel Zeit damit und wünschte ich könnte es mehr tun, aber damit kann ich leider nicht meine Rechnungen bezahlen. Finanziell haben meine Schriftarten keinen Platz in meiner Arbeit, aber sie machen einen großen Teil meiner Person aus.

Mit der Ausnahme der Elvis Schriftarten, sind alle Ihre Schriften kostenlos. Gibt es dafür einen bestimmten Grund?
S: Nicht alle Schriften sind gratis. Ich habe mehr „kommerzielle Fonts", die beinahe fertig sind, aber ich scheine nie Zeit zu haben, sie fertig zu stellen

und richtig zu veröffentlichen. Seit Jahren sage ich schon: „nächsten Sommer (oder Winter, wenn es Sommer ist), nehme ich ein paar Monate frei, um meine Fonts fertig zu bekommen". Aber es gelingt mir einfach nicht. Viele der kostenlosen Fonts sind einfach ein paar schlechte Experimente, die ich nicht ernsthaft verkaufen könnte – es gibt darunter sogar ein paar alte gepauste Exemplare. Es waren alles Schriften, die ich für einen Designauftrag gemacht habe und mich später entschieden hatte, auf meine Website zu stellen. Ich war nur bei einigen wirklich mit Leib und Seele dabei und ich wünschte ich hätte die Zeit, sie in etwas richtig Gutes zu verwandeln! Ich bin aber nicht unbedingt ein Verfechter von gratis Fonts. In der Tat, die Welt ist voll von hässlichen Designs, die von Leuten gemacht werden, die keine Ahnung von Design haben und glauben, dass sie nur mit einem Rechner umgehen können müssen. Das einzige, was sie dann machen, ist kostenlose Sachen vom Web zu pflücken und zusammen zu kleben. Ich habe nichts dagegen, dass sie das tun – es freut mich, dass es ihnen Spaß macht – aber das Problem ist, dass viele Kunden zu glauben beginnen, dies wäre die Art und Weise in der Grafikdesign vor sich geht. Andererseits generiert das Verschenken von Dingen Besucher, was wiederum Respekt einbringen oder zu neuen Kunden führen könnte. Es kann dich ebenfalls in Kontakt mit Kollegen oder Musikern bringen, die deinen Font für eine CD verwenden und dir dann eine Kopie davon schicken. Alles gut!

Entwerfen Sie ebenfalls Schriften ohne dabei eine bestimmte Anwendung vor Augen zu haben oder werden diese nur für Ihre eigenen Anforderungen als ein Designer bzw. Illustrator gemacht?
S: Ja, das tue ich, aber ich gebe diese Schriften nicht gratis weg. Das Produzieren von Schriften ist sehr aufwendig und die Verwendung von bestimmten Fonts kann einem Designer einen gewissen Grad von Exklusivität verleihen. Es ist mir lieber, dass meine Schriften in einer netten Weise verwendet werden, anstatt dass sie missbraucht werden, aber ich habe zu viel zu tun, um meine Schriften in der richtigen Art und Weise zu verkaufen. Es ist besser, dass das Produzieren von Fonts etwas ist, das mir große Freude macht als dass es zu einem Beruf wird, der mir Kopfschmerzen bereitet. Manchmal, wenn ich so etwas wie eine Broschüre entwerfe oder ein kleines Büchlein oder was auch immer, scheint es einfacher zu sein, einen kleinen Font zu erstellen (oder alte Muster einzuscannen und in eine Schrift umzuwandeln) als meine gesamte Fontsammlung zu durchsuchen, um die richtige Schrift zu finden. Ich gebe viele von diesen Fonts als kostenlose Fonts weg.

Erstellen Sie Ihre Schriften aus der Ansicht eines Grafikdesigners oder der eines Illustrators?
S: Mein „kommerzieller Typ" ist persönlicher, genau wie meine Illustrationsarbeiten. Ich versuche, die Kurven, das Gefühl, die Bewegung so ansprechend wie in meinen Illustrations- und Animationsarbeiten zu machen. Das ist etwas worum ich, im Gegensatz zu meiner Designarbeit, nicht gefragt werde. Dort muss man die Anforderungen des Kunden erfüllen. Das bedeutet nicht, dass der Designer etwas macht nach dem der Kunde fragt; in dieser Position muss ich manchmal den Kunden auch vor etwas warnen. Ich denke, wenn Kunst am einen Ende des Spektrums steht und Design am anderen Ende, befindet sich Illustration genau in der Mitte. Eine Illustration ist voll mit persönlichen Entscheidungen, aber sie muss die Geschichte des Kunden erzählen. Andererseits hat das Entwerfen von Schrift einen großen Einfluss auf meine Illustrationsarbeit. Meine Arbeit ist zu sauber. Meine Kurven sind enger als sie es sein müssten. In einer Illustration ist dies nicht weiter schlimm, aber in einer Animation ist dies zu zeitaufwendig. Aber ich kann nicht widerstehen, eine Kurve in einer Zeichnung zu korrigieren, auch wenn sie nur für 1/25 einer Sekunde sichtbar ist.

Entrevues (FR)

Il n'a pas fallu à Jos Buivenga plus que ces deux dernières années pour se faire un nom en tant que nouveau talent dans le monde des créateurs de fontes. Ses magnifiques fontes libres ont tout d'abord créé la surprise et suscité l'admiration et sa nouvelle fonte commerciale, Museo, figure parmi les meilleures ventes du site MyFonts. Lorsque j'ai décidé d'utiliser son type de caractères Anivers, Jos Buivenga m'a généreusement proposé d'en élargir la palette en terminant les variantes italique et gras. Il est maintenant temps de connaître un peu mieux ce Néerlandais.

Vos fontes sont considérées comme parmi les meilleures fontes disponibles. Elles sont d'une qualité équivalente aux fontes commerciales et elles contiennent autant de séries de caractères. Pourquoi les mettre à disposition gratuitement ?
JB : Je n'avais rien calculé lorsque j'ai créé ma première fonte, Delicious. J'étais simplement fasciné par l'impression que cela ferait d'écrire un texte avec une fonte que j'aurais créée. Étant donné que je n'avais pas fait d'études dans ce domaine, le véritable défi a été de découvrir tous les pièges et de trouver les solutions appropriées pour arriver à une fonte d'allure acceptable et qui soit utilisable : Delicious. L'idée de la vendre ne m'a jamais traversé l'esprit... j'étais simplement content qu'elle plaise et que d'autres personnes aient envie de l'utiliser. Ce n'est que dix ans après que j'ai décidé de créer une autre fonte. Fontin avait encore un côté exploration typographique, et j'ai préféré la partager plutôt que de la commercialiser. Peu de temps après avoir terminé Fontin, mes fontes ont figuré parmi les « 25 meilleures fontes libres » et c'est alors que les choses ont vraiment commencé à décoller. De plus en plus de personnes m'ont découvert ainsi que mes fontes et les réactions ont été stimulantes. À tel point qu'à chaque fois que j'ai créé une nouvelle fonte, j'ai décidé de la laisser en libre accès.

Avec Museo et la nouvelle version d'Anivers, vous avez décidé d'adopter une approche différente. Certaines graisses de ces fontes peuvent être téléchargées gratuitement et les autres peuvent être acquises moyennant une faible participation. Quelle a été la cause de ce changement ?
JB : Je travaillais cinq jours par semaine depuis environ douze ans. Je souhaitais avoir plus de temps pour créer des fontes et l'an dernier, lorsque j'ai changé d'emploi et que j'ai pu travailler un jour de moins par semaine, j'en ai profité. J'ai alors décidé de proposer des fontes payantes afin de compenser financièrement ce jour.

Pouvez-vous décrire le processus de création d'une nouvelle fonte ?
JB : Je fais beaucoup de croquis. La plupart sont inutilisables, mais cela n'a pas d'importance, parce que j'aime beaucoup cette étape. Je me sers généralement de mes croquis comme point de départ pour une nouvelle fonte, mais le véritable processus de création se déroule à l'écran. Je commence toujours par les caractères minuscules (a, c, e, f, g, h, i, n, s et v) pour me donner une idée de la nouvelle fonte. Si ces caractères me plaisent, je termine les autres caractères minuscules et souvent, pendant cette étape, je fabrique les capitales H et O pour voir comment tous les caractères pourront fonctionner ensemble. Lorsque je prévois de créer également des variantes italique et gras, je réalise rapidement quelques essais préliminaires pour vérifier s'il est nécessaire d'apporter des modifications au style normal pour que toutes les variantes et les graisses fonctionnent. Généralement, je détermine approximativement les contreformes lorsque je travaille sur chaque trait et j'effectue ensuite quelques ajustements jusqu'à ce que l'espacement soit satisfaisant. C'est alors le moment d'effectuer

le crénage et d'approfondir les essais de la fonte dans diverses situations. Une fois que tout cela est terminé, je crée la version bêta finale afin d'effectuer les essais de compatibilité sur différents systèmes et avec différentes applications. Enfin, lorsque tout fonctionne comme prévu, je publie la nouvelle fonte.

Quels sont vos projets pour l'avenir ?
JB : Je travaille actuellement sur la fonte Museo Sans, destinée à compléter la police Museo. Et puis il y a Calluna, ma première tentative sérieuse de créer un type de caractères de texte. Enfin et surtout : DeliciousX et Fontin Serif attendent toujours d'être terminées et je dois mettre à jour Fontin (Semi) et Fontin Sans afin qu'elles puissent prendre en charge davantage de langues. Une nouvelle idée surgit souvent pendant que je travaille sur un projet (comme par exemple Calluna lorsque que je travaillais sur Museo) et, dans ce cas, je fais une pause dans le projet en cours pour voir si cette nouvelle idée mérite d'être développée. Ça se passe toujours de manière naturelle et je n'ai jamais à m'inquiéter de ce que je vais faire après. Parfois, j'aimerais pouvoir me couper en trois pour pouvoir terminer tout ce que je veux faire.

Janusz Marian Nowacki

Pendant longtemps, j'ai cherché une version numérique de ma police de caractères métallique polonaise préférée : Antykwa Półtawskiego. Après avoir demandé autour de moi, j'ai appris qu'une organisation s'appelant GUST (un groupe d'utilisateurs polonais du logiciel libre de création de fontes TeX) la proposait gratuitement sur son site. La qualité était très bonne et sur le même site on pouvait trouver d'autres polices de caractères reprenant soigneusement les anciennes polices de caractères métal-liques polonaises. Elles avaient toutes un point commun : Janusz Marian Nowacki.**

Comment avez-vous eu l'idée de numériser les types de caractères polonais ?
JMN : Le premier ordinateur a fait son apparition sur mon bureau en 1990. Cela a coïncidé avec le changement de système politique en Pologne. J'avais alors quarante ans et c'est ainsi que j'ai commencé mon aventure avec les ordinateurs. Jusque là, je n'y connaissais rien. J'ai dû tout apprendre à partir de zéro. Je suis journaliste de métier. Je passais alors beaucoup de temps à l'imprimerie pour surveiller la composition du journal pour lequel je travaillais avant que la loi martiale ne soit imposée (en 1981). Ce travail m'a permis de bien connaître les bases de la typographie et de rencontrer des compositeurs expérimentés. J'ai aussi appris à connaître les différentes polices de caractères polonaises. Lorsque je suis passé à l'ordinateur, j'ai été déçu en ce qui concerne la typographie. Certes, la composition assistée par ordinateur semblait moins compliquée et offrait de nouvelles possibilités. Cependant, je ne pouvais pas utiliser mes polices de caractères polonaises préférées. Les seules polices disponibles étaient Times, Helvetica et Courier. Si vous souhaitiez en utiliser une autre, il y avait deux possibilités : l'acheter ou la créer soi-même. Comme il n'existait aucune police de caractères polonaise sur le marché, j'ai dû choisir la deuxième solution.

Pouvez-vous me dire comment vous avez commencé à dessiner des caractères ?
JMN : Mes premières tentatives de créer des caractères étaient tellement primitives et ratées que je préfère ne pas en parler. J'ai vraiment commencé à travailler sérieusement sur la création de fontes avec la première version d'Antykwa Toruńska en 1994. J'ai dessiné chaque lettre avec CorelDraw, puis je les ai importées dans Fontographer. Le résultat semblait réussi, mais il s'est avéré par la

suite que beaucoup de choses laissaient à désirer. Créer des caractères ne consiste pas seulement à trouver de belles formes ; à cela s'ajoute une grande quantité de problèmes techniques qui ne font pas partie du travail habituel d'un graphiste.

Qu'avez-vous utilisé comme matériau source pour la numérisation ? Je sais que pour la fonte Antykwa Toruńska vous avez pu avoir accès aux dessins originaux.

JMN : Pour la première version, j'ai utilisé un catalogue de la fonderie Warszawska Odlewnia Czcionek (Fonderie de caractères de Varsovie). Après avoir préparé l'ébauche d'Antykwa Toruńska, j'ai rendu visite à son créateur, Zygfryd Gardzielewski, avec une énorme pile d'impressions. Nous avons discuté de chaque lettre et j'ai révisé mes idées. Zygfryd Gardzielewski a accepté l'idée de produire ses fontes. Il savait que c'était le seul moyen de conserver son travail en vie étant donné que les changements dans les technologies d'impression indiquaient que seules les fontes utilisables sur des ordinateurs allaient survivre. Comme cadeau d'adieu, il m'a donné tous les dessins qu'ils possédaient encore. J'ai dû recommencer mon travail, mais cette fois avec un matériau source de meilleure qualité. J'ai continué à consulter Zygfryd Gardzielewski jusqu'à sa mort en 2001. Après son décès, il m'a fallu résoudre les problèmes de dessin tout seul.

Vous avez décidé de développer le nombre de glyphes des polices de caractères bien au-delà du nombre de langues qu'elles couvraient à l'origine...

JMN : Les polices de caractères originales d'Antykwa Toruńska permettaient seulement de composer des textes dans un petit nombre de langues utilisant les caractères romains : le polonais, l'allemand, le français et l'anglais. Aucune autre langue n'était nécessaire en Pologne lorsque ces polices de caractères ont été créées, dans les années cinquante. Dans la première version

publiée, j'ai ajouté des lettres accentuées ainsi que différents caractères nécessaires pour la composition sur ordinateur et n'existant pas dans la version d'origine. Le format de base des fontes était le format PostScript Type1, qui ne permettait pas de créer plus de 256 caractères. J'ai pu aller plus loin avec l'apparition du format OpenType et j'ai alors commencé à travailler sur des caractères que Zygfryd Gardzielewski n'avait jamais traités. J'ai créé des lettres grecques et cyrilliques, des symboles mathématiques et une série de caractères romains qui rendaient possible la composition de textes dans des langues très exotiques, telles que le vietnamien ou le navajo. Bien sûr, tout cela n'a pas du tout été facile car je ne suis pas graphiste de métier. Les utilisateurs peuvent juger mon travail par eux-mêmes.

Compte tenu de tout le temps que vous avez dû passer sur ces projets, pourquoi avez-vous décidé de mettre vos fontes gratuitement à la disposition des utilisateurs ?

JMN : Si j'avais su que la création de fontes comportait autant de difficultés et de pièges techniques, je n'aurais sans doute jamais commencé. J'ai néanmoins réussi à surmonter les problèmes qui se sont présentés et cela m'a apporté une grande satisfaction. Je travaille essentiellement sur des fontes créées par des Polonais. En tant que nation, il semble que nous ne sommes pas très doués pour faire notre promotion et cela ne facilite pas la distribution de nos produits dans le monde. C'est ainsi que j'ai décidé de ne pas les rendre payantes. Ça leur donne une chance d'être mieux connues. Je considère que les polices de caractères polonaises appartiennent au patrimoine mondial et j'aimerais qu'elles soient utilisées par ceux qui s'y intéressent.

FontStruct

Au début de l'année 2008, un nouveau logiciel de création de fontes a été lancé sur le Web. Ce petit logiciel habile du nom de FontStruct a pris d'assaut la communauté des typographes et des graphistes. Son utilisation est gratuite et ses producteurs encouragent les utilisateurs à partager les fontes qu'ils créent. Pour en savoir plus sur FontStruct, j'ai rencontré son créateur, Rob Meek, et son sponsor, Stephen Coles, directeur typographique de FontShop International.

Comment vous est venue l'idée de créer FontStruct ?

RM : FontStruct est né d'une longue fascination pour les fontes modulaires. Les fontes modulaires sont amusantes et relativement simples à créer, idéales pour celui ou celle qui aime jouer avec des systèmes et dans certaines limites. De plus, je pense que ces fontes sont un bon point de départ pour se lancer dans la création typographique. FontStruct a été conçu comme un outil pour développer de telles fontes. C'est un outil d'utilisation simple et non technique. Il a aussi hérité de ma série d'outils de création de fontes ludiques et conviviaux « MEEK Typographic Synthesizers ». Les « MEEK Typographic Synthesizers » sont des outils qui permettent de s'initier en s'amusant. Avec FontStruct, j'ai voulu essayer de développer quelque chose d'utile et susceptible d'intéresser un public plus large.

De quelle manière la société FontShop s'est engagée dans le développement de FontStruct ?

SC : Une longue et étroite collaboration s'était déjà créée entre FontShop et Rob Meek, en travaillant sur plusieurs améliorations du site FontShop. com. Rob Meek nous a présenté le concept de FontStruct et nous a demandé d'être son sponsor et de coproduire le site.

Avez-vous eu dès le départ l'idée de baser FontStruct sur le Web ?

RM : Oui. Je pense que les fontes sont particulièrement bien adaptées à la création en ligne et au partage, caractéristiques d'une nouvelle époque. Les tailles de fichier relativement petites et l'espace de création clairement structuré se prêtent à la création basée sur un navigateur. J'espère que FontStruct pourra devenir une sorte de mini-Flickr/Picnik pour le monde des fontes modulaires.

Pour vous, quelle est la raison d'être de FontStruct ?

SC : Il n'est pas de meilleur moyen d'améliorer sa connaissance des caractères typographiques et des outils nécessaires pour les créer que de mettre la main à la pâte. C'est pour cela que dessiner des lettres est un exercice fréquent dans les écoles professionnelles de typographie et de graphisme. FontStruct fait partie de la mission de FontShop visant à développer la connaissance des caractères typographiques en général et à mieux valoriser les fontes numériques de qualité aux yeux du public. La création et le partage de fontes est un excellent moyen de se rapprocher de cet objectif et l'accès libre est essentiel pour l'existence d'une communauté ouverte et épanouie.

RM : Pour ma part, j'espère que c'est une introduction agréable au plaisir de la création typographique pour les débutants, et un terrain de jeu pour les adeptes des fontes modulaires plus expérimentés.

Le fait d'encourager les utilisateurs de FontStruct à mettre leurs fontes gratuitement à disposition ne crée-t-il pas une concurrence avec les fontes modulaires que vous vendez vous-même ?

SC : FontStructor (l'outil d'édition de FontStruct) offre à l'utilisateur un niveau de flexibilité surprenant, comme le montrent les fontes actuellement exposées dans la « galerie ». Alors oui, le téléchargement gratuit peut être considéré comme un pari pour un marchand de fontes. Cependant, les limitations de la grille ne permettent pas vraiment de créer des fontes de niveau professionnel. En fin de compte, avec FontStruct nous soutenons une communauté mondiale de passionnés de fontes qui ne peut que bénéficier à FontShop et à l'industrie dans son ensemble.

Rob, vous avez aussi utilisé FontStruct pour créer deux fontes présentées en illustration dans ce livre. Votre passion est-elle de créer des fontes ou plutôt de créer les outils pour permettre à d'autres de le faire ?
RM : Sans aucun doute la deuxième. Le fait d'avoir une certaine expérience comme graphiste et typographe amateur, ainsi que comme développeur, m'a incontestablement aidé dans ce projet, mais j'ai aussi beaucoup de respect pour les personnes qui possèdent une passion authentique pour la typographie. Voir les choses incroyables que d'autres ont réussi à faire avec cet outil est une grande récompense pour moi.

Essayez vous-même :
fontstruct.fontshop.com

Brode Vosloo

Brode Vosloo a acquis une certaine notoriété avec ses fontes qui essaient de reproduire l'esprit africain de façon authentique et réaliste. Elles n'ont rien à voir avec les fontes stéréotypées utilisées par les entreprises de tourisme pour représenter ce continent. Il a puisé son inspiration directement dans les caractères que l'on voit dans la rue. Son ancienne fonderie de caractères « The Sacred Nipple » a été très remarquée et Brode Vosloo a également produit des fontes pour T.26, la fonderie américaine culte de Carlos Segura. Puis tout s'est calmé.

La plupart de vos fontes ont été publiées en tant que fontes libres. Pourquoi n'avez-vous pas plutôt décidé

de les publier comme fontes payantes ?
BV : Bien que j'aie étudié le graphisme dans l'une des institutions les plus réputées en Afrique du Sud, je n'ai pas eu l'occasion d'étudier avec un maître de la typographie ni d'utiliser des logiciels de création de fontes tels que Fontographer. Pour créer des fontes fonctionnelles, j'ai dû apprendre par moi-même tout ce que je pouvais sur la typographie et sur les logiciels de création de fontes. Les premières fontes que j'ai créées étaient des tentatives expérimentales pour accéder au monde de la typographie et honnêtement, je ne pensais pas qu'elles méritaient que l'on paie pour les utiliser. En poursuivant mon voyage typographique, j'ai pris conscience du besoin de disposer de fontes spécifiquement africaines, des caractères qui reflètent le côté sableux et l'énergie des rues africaines, des caractères qui se distinguent de ces fontes pour touristes de mauvais goût qui sont actuellement utilisées pour représenter l'Afrique. C'est ainsi que les fontes libres iAlfabhethi, iZulu, Mr CV Joint, Pleine Str., Rural et Star Salon ont vu le jour. Avec les conseils de Carlos Segura, j'ai ensuite créé des polices de caractères payantes avec toutes les séries de caractères, comme les collections Shoe Repairs et Freeline et la fonte « pâté » Afrodisiac. Ces fontes sont actuellement distribuées par la fonderie T.26 de Carlos Segura.

Pourquoi avez-vous cessé de créer des fontes libres ?
BV : À la fin des années quatre-vingt-dix, on avait l'impression qu'il suffisait d'un ordinateur et d'un logiciel de création de fontes pour être un typographe. Cela a donné naissance à de nombreuses fontes libres, et ce phénomène existe probablement encore aujourd'hui. Souvent, ces fontes ne sont que des réinterprétations de fontes créées au milieu des années quatre-vingt-dix par d'autres graphistes. J'ai commencé à trouver que tout ce qui était mis à disposition gratuitement sur Internet était sans valeur. Après avoir publié

ma fonte Shoe Repairs, je connaissais d'une part la peine et le plaisir qui accompagnent le travail ardu que représente la création d'une police de caractère complète et fonctionnelle et, d'autre part, j'étais attristé de voir que les utilisateurs préféraient les fontes libres aux fontes créées par des maîtres de la typographie. Même les fontes les plus simples demandent de la prévoyance et de l'huile de coude, deux aspects pour lesquels la création de fonte mérite à mes yeux d'être rémunérée. Mais cela ne veut pas dire que je sois totalement opposé aux fontes libres. Je continue à penser que l'ordinateur a mis la création de fontes à la portée de tous les graphistes et que cela a permis à des idées incroyables de voir le jour. Les fontes libres ont certainement apporté un souffle d'air frais à une profession qui était réservée à une toute petite élite. Je pense que les fontes de bonne qualité finissent toujours par remonter en haut du panier.

Cela fait déjà longtemps que vous avez publié votre dernière police de caractères. Cela correspond-il à un changement de direction dans votre travail ?
BV : Cela fait effectivement un certain temps que je n'ai pas publié de nouvelle fonte. Ceci est principalement dû au fait que j'ai abordé d'autres domaines comme le dessin animé et le dessin de mode et que je ne travaille plus uniquement dans le milieu du graphisme pur. Je continue malgré tout à noter des idées de nouvelles fontes et à les utiliser dans mon travail. Je travaille actuellement dans le secteur des sports d'action pour une marque qui a commencé avec le motocross et qui est actuellement sérieusement engagée dans les sports et loisirs tels que le BMX, le surf et la planche nautique. Je suis leur directeur marketing et ce travail est idéal pour moi, car il me permet de mettre à profit mon expérience dans le graphisme et la communication et de vivre mon engagement dans les sports d'action. La plupart des idées de nouvelles fontes sur lesquelles je travaille s'inspirent de ce style de

vie : des fontes grasses à la mode qui peuvent trouver leur place sur les cadres de vélo ou les planches de surf, qui peuvent être découpées dans le vinyle, brodées ou gravées ; des fontes inspirées par les tatouages ou les scarifications et qui peuvent être facilement reproduites ; des fontes qui passent bien sur les écrans et qui peuvent être animées tout en conservant une bonne lisibilité. Bien que je puise mes idées de création de nouvelles fontes dans des sources très diverses, je pense qu'une nouvelle idée doit répondre à au moins un de mes quatre critères pour valoir la peine de la transformer en une nouvelle fonte entièrement fonctionnelle : elle doit être intemporelle, conceptuelle, fonctionnelle ou liée à la texture. Je suis sûr que le temps viendra où j'aurai assez de temps pour créer de nouvelles fontes, mais en attendant ce moment, je vais continuer à rouler sur mon VTT et à surfer tout mon soûl, lorsque je ne suis pas en train de travailler. Je pense que si une fonte est vraiment exceptionnelle, cela n'a pas d'importance qu'elle soit publiée maintenant ou bien dans dix ans. En attendant, je vais continuer à noter mes idées et à mettre à profit ces années pour filtrer les idées qui ne valent pas la peine et profiter des superbes fontes qui existent déjà.

Lopetz – Büro Destruct

Le studio Büro Destruct est à la pointe du graphisme moderne en Suisse depuis le milieu des années quatre-vingt-dix. Le travail de ses membres a influencé des graphistes dans le monde entier, après la parution de deux livres, publiés par la maison d'édition « Die Gestalten Verlag ». Dès ses débuts, les membres de Büro Destruct ont créé des polices de caractères correspondant à leur style original et ont décidé d'en partager gratuitement une bonne partie avec d'autres graphistes.

Lorsque vous avez commencé à créer les premières fontes Büro Destruct pour les besoins de votre propre travail, vous les avez immédiatement mises à disposition du public, ce que vous continuez à faire...
L : La création de fontes a toujours joué un rôle important dans notre travail. La raison principale de créer des fontes originales sur mesure est de pouvoir parler un seul et même langage dans notre travail quotidien de graphistes. La deuxième raison est de rendre ces fontes publiques afin de pouvoir les partager avec d'autres graphistes.

Comment décidez-vous qu'une police de caractères sera publiée comme fonte libre ou comme fonte commerciale ?
L : C'est en fonction de la quantité de travail qu'a demandé la création de cette fonte. Pour la plupart, les fontes libres sont des fontes dont la création n'a pas pris trop de temps. Plus la fonte est « professionnelle » (travail de crénage, différents styles, lisibilité), plus elle a de chances de devenir une fonte payante. On évalue aussi le degré d'utilité de la fonte. Si nous pensons que la fonte peut être utilisée pour la publicité d'une grande entreprise avec un gros budget, on tombe alors dans la catégorie des fontes payantes.

Vous êtes un studio de création graphique renommé. Pensez-vous que cela permet à vos fontes d'être prises plus au sérieux par les autres graphistes ?
L : Notre statut bénéficie assurément à nos fontes libres ainsi qu'à nos fontes payantes. Mais nous voyons cela autrement : nos fontes nous ont aidé à devenir un « studio de création graphique renommé ». Comparées à celles d'autres créateurs, nos fontes peuvent être considérées comme moins sérieuses, mais cela est inhérent à leur nature, à l'esprit dans lequel elles sont créées. Pour nous, la création de fontes est plutôt une expérience et un jeu qu'un travail ardu et précis. Notre but n'est pas de créer une nouvelle police Helvetica, Garamond ou autre : il faudrait des années pour y parvenir.

Nous voulons créer de nouvelles formes graphiques qui puissent être compilées en un alphabet et les publier. C'est la même chose que lorsque nous avons commencé à créer des fontes dans les premières années de Büro Destruct, à partir de 1995. Par exemple, la police flossy, notre premier travail de création de fontes, consistait simplement en une silhouette de mouton prenant des poses représentant les différents caractères.

Pouvez-vous me parler du processus de création que vous suivez lorsque vous créez vos fontes ? Est-ce que vous créez une fonte parce que vous avez une idée de nouvelle fonte ou bien parce que vous travaillez sur un projet pour lequel vous sentez le besoin de créer une nouvelle fonte ?
L : Généralement, une nouvelle fonte Büro Destruct voit le jour après la création d'un logo, d'un titre pour une affiche de concert ou un prospectus, ou encore une couverture de CD. Le meilleur exemple est la fonte BD Balduin, qui vient du logo que nous avons créé pour le musicien Balduin. Parfois, une nouvelle fonte vient d'une forme que nous aimons et que nous décidons d'explorer sur tout l'alphabet. Une source importante d'inspiration est de voyager dans d'autres pays utilisant d'autres langues qui s'écrivent avec des caractères autres que les caractères romains, comme par exemple les caractères japonais, arabes, etc. Nous ne savons pas les lire ; nous observons seulement leur forme et nous les réutilisons ensuite dans nos alphabets.

Réutilisez-vous souvent vos propres fontes dans votre travail de graphiste ?
L : Notre idée est de les utiliser lorsque c'est logique, étant donné qu'elles parlent notre propre langage, mais souvent nous finissons par utiliser d'autres fontes. La raison principale est que les fontes que nous créons sont toujours associées à un projet déterminé ou à une idée précise. Elles appartiennent à ce projet ou cette idée et à cette période. Nous partageons nos nouvelles fontes

avec d'autres graphistes et il est intéressant et surprenant pour nous de voir comment ils utilisent nos fontes dans leur propre contexte.

Shamrock

Shamrock (a.k.a. Jeroen Klaver) est surtout connu pour ses superbes illustrations à l'ambiance rétro. Peu de gens savent qu'il a obtenu une licence en arts graphiques et qu'il a créé des fontes libres ainsi que des fontes commercia-les. Beaucoup de ses fontes reflètent son style de dessin, parce que la plupart d'entre elles sont créées spécifiquement pour ses propres illustrations. Lorsqu'on utilise les fontes de Shamrock, on transfert aussi un peu de son esprit artistique. Elles sont amusantes, animées et irrésistibles.

Je connaissais vos illustrations mais pas vraiment vos fontes. Quelle place vos fontes prennent-elles dans votre travail ?
S : Une place importante. J'ai commencé comme graphiste parce que j'ai toujours aimé fabriquer des choses comme des fanzines et des prospectus. Je ne suis pas le genre de graphiste qui se contente de positionner une image et d'ajouter un peu de texte en haut. J'aime réaliser les choses comme un tout. Tout doit être bien fait et doit s'équilibrer. J'attache aussi beaucoup d'importance au texte. Il m'est arrivé de refuser des travaux parce que le texte n'avait pas de sens. Lorsque l'on fait tout soi-même, on est libre de faire ce qu'on veut ! De plus, la manière avec laquelle les choses sont faites m'intéresse. Je sais qu'il existe des personnes qui peuvent faire certaines choses bien mieux que moi mais le fait d'essayer par moi-même me donne beaucoup de respect pour ces personnes et facilite la communication avec elles.
J'ai commencé à dessiner des lettres sérieusement

lorsque j'étais au lycée. J'ai passé beaucoup de temps à cela et j'aurais aimé en passer encore plus, mais ce travail ne suffit pas à nourrir son homme. Ainsi, financièrement parlant, mes fontes n'ont aucune place dans mon travail mais elles sont une grande partie de ce que je pense être.

À l'exception d'Elvis, toutes vos fontes sont des fontes libres. Y a-t-il une raison précise à cela ?
S : Toutes les fontes ne sont pas libres. J'ai créé d'autres « fontes commerciales » qui sont presque terminées mais je n'arrive pas à trouver le temps pour le faire et les publier correctement. Pendant des années je me suis dit : « l'été prochain (ou l'hiver quand c'était l'été) je prendrai quelques mois de congés pour mettre mes affaires en ordre ». Mais je ne suis jamais parvenu à le faire. Beaucoup de fontes libres sont de simples expériences ratées, que je ne pourrais pas vendre en restant sérieux : il y a même quelques vieux spécimens décalqués parmi elles. Toutes les fontes libres sont des fontes que j'ai créées pour un projet particulier et que j'ai ensuite décidé de mettre à disposition sur mon site. J'en aime vraiment seulement quelques-unes et j'aimerais avoir le temps d'en faire quelque chose de bien ! Je ne suis pas un partisan des fontes libres en soi. En fait, je pense que le monde est envahi de graphismes laids, faits par des gens qui ne savent pas dessiner et qui pensent qu'il suffit de savoir utiliser un ordinateur. La seule chose qu'ils savent faire est de récupérer des trucs gratuits sur le Web et de les coller ensemble. Cela ne me dérange pas, je suis content s'ils trouvent du plaisir à le faire, mais le mauvais côté est que de nombreux clients commencent à croire que c'est comme cela que fonctionne la création graphique. D'un autre côté, le fait de distribuer des cadeaux attire des visiteurs, et cela peut apporter de la reconnaissance ou de nouveaux clients. C'est aussi un moyen d'être en contact avec des collègues ou des musiciens qui utilisent une fonte pour un CD et qui vous en envoient un exemplaire. Tout le monde est content !

Vous arrive-t-il de créer des fontes sans avoir une application précise à l'esprit, ou sont-elles toujours faites pour répondre à vos besoins de graphiste/ illustrateur ?

S : Oui, cela m'arrive, mais je ne distribue pas ce genre de fontes gratuitement. La fabrication des fontes représente beaucoup de travail et l'utilisation d'une fonte particulière peut apporter au graphiste un peu d'exclusivité. Je préfère que mes fontes soient utilisées correctement plutôt que maltraitées, mais je suis trop occupé pour accorder le temps nécessaire à les commercialiser efficacement. Je préfère que la création de fontes demeure un plaisir pour moi plutôt que cela se transforme en une profession qui me donne des maux de tête. Parfois, lorsque je réalise un projet tel qu'une brochure ou une plaquette, il m'arrive de trouver plus facile de créer une petite fonte (ou de scanner d'anciens spécimens et de les transformer en fonte) plutôt que de parcourir toutes mes fontes pour en trouver une qui convienne. J'en distribue ensuite la plupart comme fontes libres.

Créez-vous vos fontes avec le regard d'un graphiste ou celui d'un illustrateur ?

S : Mes « fontes commerciales » sont un travail plus personnel, à la manière de mes illustrations. J'essaie de rendre les courbes, l'impression, le mouvement aussi agréables pour moi que je le fais dans mon travail d'illustration ou d'animation. C'est quelque chose que personne ne me demande de faire, à la différence d'un travail de graphisme, où l'on doit répondre aux besoins du client. Cela ne signifie pas que le graphiste exécute ce que le client lui demande. Dans ce genre de situation je dois parfois déconseiller aux clients de suivre leurs idées. Je pense que si l'on met l'art d'un côté et le graphisme de l'autre, l'illustration se trouve exactement à mi-chemin entre les deux. C'est une activité qui demande beaucoup de décisions personnelles mais qui doit néanmoins raconter l'histoire du client. D'un autre côté, la création

de fontes a une grande influence sur mon travail d'illustrateur. Je travaille trop proprement. Toutes mes courbes sont beaucoup plus précises que nécessaire. Pour l'illustration, ce n'est pas si mal, mais pour l'animation, ça me prend énormément de temps. Je ne peux simplement pas m'empêcher de corriger une courbe dans un dessin, même si elle est seulement visible pendant 1/25e de seconde !

Entrevistas (ES)

Jos Buivenga — exljbris

Jos Buivenga ha despuntado en el último par de años como nuevo talento en el campo del diseño tipográfico. Lo primero que hizo fue crear letras gratuitas de una belleza pasmosa. Y ahora ha lanzado su primera tipografía comercial, Museo, una de las más vendidas según la lista de MyFonts. Cuando decidí componer el texto de este libro con su tipografía Anivers, Jos tuvo la deferencia de ultimar la Anivers cursiva y negrita para ampliar la paleta tipográfica. Es hora de conocer un poco mejor a este holandés.

Tus fuentes están consideradas de las mejores disponibles de forma gratuita. Su calidad es equiparable a la de muchas tipografías comerciales existentes en el mercado y, además, contienen juegos de caracteres igual de extensos que estas. ¿Por qué decidiste distribuirlas gratis?

JB: Cuando creé mi primera tipografía, Delicious, no tenía ningún plan en mente. Simplemente me fascinaba la idea de componer un texto con una tipografía de creación propia. Puesto que yo no había estudiado diseño tipográfico, el verdadero desafío fue descubrir todos los entresijos y dar con las soluciones pertinentes para obtener un tipo propio que funcionara a nivel estético y práctico. Así nació Delicious. Jamás se me ocurrió ponerla a la venta… Me encantaba que a otras personas les gustara y la quisieran utilizar. Tardé diez años en decidir crear otra. Fontin también fue una exploración tipográfica, de modo que preferí compartirla en lugar de venderla. Poco después de finalizar Fontin, mis tipografías aparecieron en la lista de Vitaly Friedman de las «25 fuentes gratuitas de mejor calidad». Fue entonces cuando la cosa empezó a despegar de verdad. Muchas personas me conocieron y descubrieron mis fuentes gratuitas y obtuve una respuesta muy alentadora… tanto que decidí distribuir gratuitamente todas las que creara.

Sin embargo, en el caso de Museo y de la nueva versión de la Anivers decidiste adoptar un enfoque distinto. Algunos de los grosores de la familia tipográfica pueden descargarse de forma gratuita mientras que otros se adquieren por una pequeña suma. ¿Qué te impulsó a incorporar ese cambio?

JB: Trabajo cinco días a la semana desde hace doce años. Me apetecía tener más tiempo para diseñar tipografías, así que el año pasado, cuando se me presentó la oportunidad de cambiar de empleo y trabajar un día menos por semana, me sentí inmensamente feliz. Decidí ofrecer fuentes de pago para obtener una cierta compensación económica por esa jornada laboral.

¿Podrías describir tu metodología para diseñar una tipografía?

JB: Hago un montón de borradores. La mayoría de ellos no puedo utilizarlos, pero no me importa porque disfruto haciéndolos. A menudo empleo los borradores como punto de partida, pero el proceso real tiene lugar invariablemente en la pantalla. Siempre empiezo con algunos glifos de caja baja (a, c, e, f, g, h, i, n, s y v) para tener una primera impresión de la nueva tipografía. Si me gustan, continúo creando el resto de caracteres en caja baja y, con frecuencia, mientras tanto diseño la H y la O mayúsculas para hacerme una idea global de cómo encajará todo. Si tengo previsto crear también la versión negrita y cursiva, hago algunas pruebas preliminares rápidas en sucio con vistas a comprobar si tengo que incorporar algún cambio en la redonda para garantizar que todos los grosores y estilos funcionen. Por lo general determino a grandes rasgos los espacios laterales al trabajar en cada uno de los glifos y hago varias rondas de ajustes hasta dar con el espaciado idóneo. A continuación defino el interletraje (kern) y sigo probando la tipografía con distintos usos. Una vez hecho todo esto, genero la versión beta final para poder realizar pruebas de compatibilidad en distintas plataformas y aplicaciones. Cuando obtengo el resultado deseado, publico la nueva tipografía.

¿Qué planes tienes para el futuro?
JB: Actualmente trabajo en la Museo Sans para completar la Museo. Y también tengo pendiente la Calluna, que es mi primer intento serio de hacer una tipografía para texto. Por último, pero no menos importante, aún tengo que ultimar la DeliciousX y la Fontin Serif, además de actualizar la Fontin (Semi) y la Fontin Sans con caracteres para otros idiomas. Con frecuencia se me ocurre una idea (por ejemplo, imaginé la Calluna cuando estaba trabajando en la Museo) y hago una «pausa» para investigar si merece la pena ahondar en ella o no. El proceso es siempre muy natural; de hecho, nunca me preocupo en pensar qué haré a continuación. A veces me gustaría poder multiplicarme por tres para hacer todo lo que me apetece.

Janusz Marian Nowacki

Dediqué mucho tiempo a buscar una versión digital de mi tipo de metal polaco preferido, Antykwa Półtawskiego. Tras preguntar por ahí descubrí que una organización llamada GUST (el grupo de usuarios polacos del software de diseño tipográfico gratuito llamado TeX) lo ofrecía en su sitio web de forma gratuita. Tenía una calidad muy buena y en la misma página web encontré otras versiones de tipos de metal polacos elaboradas con esmero. Todas ellas tenían algo en común: eran obra de Janusz Marian Nowacki.

¿Cómo se te ocurrió la idea de digitalizar tipografías polacas clásicas?
JMN: Tuve mi primer ordenador personal en 1990, fecha que coincidió con el cambio de sistema político en Polonia. Yo tenía entonces 40 años y así fue como empecé mi singladura en la informática.

Hasta entonces no sabía nada de ordenadores. Tuve que aprender a utilizarlos desde cero. Soy periodista de profesión y antes pasaba bastantes horas en la imprenta supervisando la fotocomposición del periódico para el que trabajaba antes de que se impusiera la ley marcial (en 1981). En aquella época fui familiarizándome con los conceptos básicos de la tipografía y conocí a tipógrafos expertos. También descubrí los tipos de metal polacos. Cuando empecé a trabajar con ordenadores, la oferta tipográfica me decepcionó. La composición de textos con ayuda del ordenador parecía menos complicada y abría nuevos horizontes. Sin embargo, no podía utilizar mis tipografías polacas preferidas. Las únicas disponibles eran la Times, la Helvetica y la Courier. Si querías aplicar algo distinto, tenías dos alternativas: comprarla o crearla. Y, puesto que no había tipografías polacas a la venta, me vi obligado a decantarme por la segunda opción.

¿Podrías explicarme cómo empezaste a diseñar tipografías?
JMN: Mis primeros intentos de diseñar tipografías fueron tan primitivos y lamentables que prefiero no mencionarlos. Calculo que empecé a trabajar en serio en la primera versión de la Antykwa Toruńska en 1994. Creé los dibujos de algunas letras con CorelDraw y luego los importé en Fontographer. Los resultados me parecieron aceptables, aunque luego se demostró que dejaban mucho que desear. Las tipografías no son únicamente letras con formas bonitas, sino que integran un montón de aspectos técnicos completamente ajenos al diseñador.

¿Qué material utilizaste para la digitalización? Me consta que tuviste acceso a los diseños originales para digitalizar la Antykwa Toruńska.
JMN: La fuente de referencia para la primera versión fue un catálogo de la Warszawska Odlewnia Czcionek (Fundición Tipográfica de Varsovia). Tras preparar el borrador de la Antykwa Toruńska, visité a su creador, Zygfryd Gardzielewski, con un montón

de pruebas de impresión. Debatimos pormenorizadamente cada letra y revisé mis ideas. Zygfryd Gardzielewski accedió a producir sus tipografías. Sabía que era el único modo de mantener su trabajo con vida, puesto que los cambios en las tecnologías de impresión implicaban que solo los formatos legibles informáticamente sobrevivirían. Como regalo de despedida me entregó todos los materiales de diseño que aún poseía. Así que tuve que empezar de nuevo, pero esta vez con una fuente de referencia gráfica infinitamente mejor. Continué consultando con Zygfryd Gardzielewski hasta su muerte en 2001. A su muerte, tuve que solventar los problemas de diseño por mí mismo.

Optaste por ampliar bastante la cantidad de glifos de las tipografías con respecto al número de idiomas que cubrían originalmente…

JMN: Las tipografías originales de la Antykwa Toruńska solo permitían componer textos en unas cuantas lenguas con abecedario latino: polaco, alemán, francés e inglés. En la época de su creación, en la década de 1950, en Polonia no se necesitaban otros idiomas. En la primera versión publicada añadí algunas letras acentuadas y algunos caracteres necesarios para la composición con ordenador que no formaban parte de la familia tipográfica metálica. El formato básico de los tipos era PostScript Type1, limitado a 256 caracteres. La aparición del formato OpenType me permitió continuar ampliando la tipografía y empecé a diseñar caracteres de los que Zygfryd Gardzielewski no se había ocupado. También creé letras griegas y cirílicas, símbolos matemáticos y un juego de letras latinas que permitía componer textos en idiomas muy exóticos, como el vietnamita o el navajo. Evidentemente, no fue tarea fácil, porque yo no soy diseñador profesional. Los usuarios pueden juzgar mi trabajo por sí mismos.

Teniendo en cuenta la cantidad de tiempo que habrás tenido que invertir en estos proyectos, ¿por

qué decidiste poner las tipografías a disposición del público de forma gratuita?

JMN: De haber sabido lo difícil que es diseñar una tipografía y la infinidad de obstáculos tecnológicos que hay que salvar, probablemente ni siquiera habría empezado. No obstante, he logrado superar los problemas que se me han planteado y ha resultado muy reconfortante. Me dedico sobre todo a tipografías diseñadas por polacos. Como nación, parece que nos falta talento para promocionarnos y eso nos dificulta dar a conocer nuestros productos al mundo. Eso fue lo que me impulsó a no cobrar por las tipografías. De este modo tal vez ganemos un poco de popularidad. Considero que las tipografías polacas forman parte del legado cultural mundial y me gusta que pueda utilizarlas quienquiera que esté interesado en ellas.

FontStruct

A principios de 2008 apareció un nuevo software de edición de fuentes en forma de página web. FontStruct, nombre de este ingenioso programilla, ha tomado la comunidad del diseño y la tipografía por asalto. De uso gratuito, sus creadores instan a los usuarios a compartir las tipografías que diseñan. Tenía que descubrir más acerca del tema, de modo que decidí charlar con su creador, Rob Meek, y con el patrocinador, Stephen Coles, a su vez director de tipografía de FontShop International.

¿De dónde nació la idea original de crear el programa FontStruct?

RM: FontStruct es el resultado de una fascinación imperecedera por las tipografías modulares. Los tipos modulares son divertidos y relativamente fáciles de crear, ideales para todas aquellas personas interesadas en jugar con sistemas y dentro de unos límites determinados. Además, opino que es un excelente punto de partida para cualquiera que quiera iniciarse en el diseño tipográfico. FontStruct se concibió como herramienta para desarrollar este tipo de fuentes. Se diseñó para que fuese fácil de usar y nada técnico. Además, comparte legado con mis sintetizadores tipográficos MEEK, un conjunto de juguetitos accesibles para diseñar tipografías. Los sintetizadores tipográficos MEEK son ejercicios divertidos, esotéricos. Mi intención al concebir FontStruct era desarrollar algo que pudiera resultar de utilidad e interés para un público más amplio.

¿Cómo se involucró FontShop en la creación de FontStruct?
SC: FontShop y Rob Meek mantenían una estrecha relación laboral desde hacía tiempo, a raíz de la cual se añadieron varias mejoras a FontShop.com. Rob nos presentó el concepto de FontStruct y nos solicitó que patrocináramos y coprodujéramos el sitio web.

¿Desde el principio tuviste la idea de poner el software a disponibilidad del público a modo de sitio web?
RM: Sí. Creo que las tipografías son especialmente idóneas para la nueva era de creación y colaboración on-line. Los tamaños relativamente pequeños de los archivos y el espacio creativo claramente estructurado se prestan a la edición desde navegadores. Espero que FontStruct se convierta en una especie de mini Flickr/Picnik para el sector de las tipografías modulares.

¿Cuál es el objetivo subyacente de FontStruct?
SC: No hay ningún modo mejor de que se valoren las tipografías y las habilidades que se requieren para su creación que probar uno mismo. Por eso el dibujo de letras a menudo forma parte de los cursos de diseño gráfico y tipográfico que se imparten en las universidades. FontStruct se une a la misión de FontShop de concienciar acerca de las tipografías en general y elevar el valor percibido de las fuentes tipográficas bien diseñadas. Crear y compartir

tipografías es un modo excelente para avanzar en este camino y dar acceso gratuito a los tipos es esencial para lograr tejer una comunidad abierta y próspera.
RM: Personalmente, espero que constituya una introducción divertida al placer de crear tipografías para los neófitos... y que dé alas a la creatividad de los amantes de las tipografías modulares más experimentados.

¿No estáis generando competencia para las tipografías modulares que vosotros mismos vendéis al alentar a los usuarios de FontStruct a distribuir sus fuentes de forma gratuita?
SC: FontStructor (el editor que incorpora FontStruct) otorga al usuario un grado de flexibilidad asombroso, tal como demuestran las tipografías expuestas actualmente en la galería. Así que, efectivamente, permitir las descargas gratuitas podría considerarse una apuesta arriesgada. Sin embargo, las limitaciones de la retícula no permiten crear tipografías profesionales. Al final, con FontStruct lo que hacemos es cultivar una comunidad global de entusiastas de la tipografía que acabará por beneficiar tanto a FontShop como al sector en su conjunto.

Rob, tú también has creado un par de tipografías con FontStruct que se recogen en este libro. ¿Te motiva más diseñar tipografías o crear las herramientas para que otros lo hagan?
RM: Sin duda alguna, lo segundo. El hecho de tener experiencia como diseñador y diletante tipográfico, y también como programador, fue de utilidad para el proyecto, pero siento un respeto reverencial por los auténticos apasionados de la tipografía. Ver las magníficas letras que otros han creado con la herramienta constituye una recompensa magnífica para mí.

Pruébelo usted mismo:
fontstruct.fontshop.com

Brode Vosloo

Brode Vosloo alcanzó la fama gracias a unas tipografías que intentan condensar la auténtica alma africana. No se parecen en absoluto a las tipografías estereotípicas que utilizan las organizaciones turísticas para representar a este continente. Su fuente de inspiración fueron las pintadas y los rótulos callejeros y la señalización vial. Su hoy desaparecida fundición tipográfica, The Sacred Nipple, fue objeto de gran atención, y Vosloo llegó a producir algunas tipografías para la fundición de culto estadounidense de Carlos Segura, T.26. Luego llegó la calma.

La mayoría de tus tipografías se han distribuido de forma gratuita. ¿Por qué decidiste desde un primer momento no ponerlas a la venta?
BV: Aunque estudié diseño gráfico en una de las instituciones más reputadas de Sudáfrica, no tuve la oportunidad de formarme con tipógrafos expertos o maestros de programas de creación tipográfica como Fontographer. Tuve que aprender de forma autodidacta todo lo que pude sobre tipografía y el software utilizado para producir fuentes funcionales. Las primeras fuentes que concebí suponían incursiones experimentales en el mundo de la tipografía y, sinceramente, no consideraba que mereciera la pena pagar por ellas. Conforme continué mi camino por la tipografía detecté la necesidad de crear tipografías africanas con un carácter más único, fuentes que conden-saran de verdad la energía de las calles africanas, fuentes que se distinguieran de las horteradas que se utilizan en el sector del turismo para representar África. Así nacieron tipografías gratuitas como iAlfabhethi, iZulu, Mr CV Joint, Pleine Str., Rural y Star Salon. Con la orientación de Carlos Segura me decidí entonces a crear tipografías de pago com-pletamente funcionales, con juegos de caracteres completos, como las colecciones de Shoe Repairs y

Freeline y la tipografía de signos especiales pi font Afrodisiac. Todas estas letras se distribuyen en la actualidad a través de la fundición T.26 de Segura.

¿Por qué dejaste de crear tipografías gratuitas?
BV: A finales de la década de 1990 daba la sen-sación de que cualquiera que dispusiera de un ordenador y un software de creación de tipografías era tipógrafo. Había, y probablemente sigue habiendo, muchas tipografías gratuitas en el mercado. A menudo estos tipos no son más que reinterpretaciones de tipografías ideadas a media-dos de la década de 1990 por otros diseñadores. Me convencí de que todo aquello que se distribuía gratuitamente a través de Internet carecía de valor. Tras lanzar la Shoe Repairs conocí en carne propia el dolor y el placer que acompaña a la ardua labor de diseñar una tipografía completa y funcional, y me entristecía ver que la gente prefería tipos gratuitos a tipos creados por tipógrafos expertos. Hasta la más sencilla de las fuentes requiere una reflexión previa e hincar los codos, dos aspectos del diseño tipográfico que en mi opinión merecen alguna remuneración económica. Espero que no se me malinterprete. No veo únicamente aspectos negati-vos en la distribución gratuita de tipografías. Soy de la opinión de que el ordenador ha puesto la creación tipográfica en manos del diseñador corriente y esto ha proporcionado oportunidades para que algunas ideas fabulosas cobren vida. Sin ningún género de dudas, las tipografías gratuitas han insuflado nueva vida a una profesión que antes estaba reservada a una élite. Supongo que las buenas tipografías, como la buena nata, siempre subirán.

Ha transcurrido mucho tiempo desde que lanzaste tu última tipografía. ¿Estás centrado en otra faceta de tu trabajo?
BV: Es cierto que ha pasado algún tiempo desde que publiqué mi última tipografía. Esto se debe en gran medida a que me aparté del entorno laboral del diseño gráfico puro para zambullirme en otras

áreas, como la animación y el diseño de moda. He continuado esbozando ideas para nuevas tipografías y las he utilizado en mi trabajo. Ahora trabajo en el sector de los deportes de acción para una marca cuyas raíces originales entroncaban con el motocross y se ha consolidado en el BMX, el surf y el esquí acuático. Soy director de marketing, un empleo que es la combinación ideal de mis habilidades de diseño y de comunicación y mi participación activa en los deportes de acción. La mayoría de las ideas para nuevas tipografías en las que he estado trabajando se inspiran en este estilo de vida: son fuentes atrevidas y modernas que pueden estamparse en el armazón de una bicicleta o en la quilla de una tabla de surf, troquelarse en vinilo, bordarse o grabarse; son tipografías inspiradas en tatuajes y escarificaciones y fáciles de replicar, tipografías que se traducen bien en pantalla y que pueden animarse fácilmente sin perder legibilidad. Aunque bebo de muchas fuentes de inspiración, cualquier idea que tenga para una nueva tipografía tiene que cumplir al menos uno de mis cuatro criterios para que considere que merece la pena diseñarla con todas su funcionalidades: tiene que ser atemporal, conceptual, funcional o textual. Estoy convencido de que llegará un día en que tendré tiempo para publicar tipografías nuevas, pero hasta entonces seguiré montando mi sucia bicicleta y surfeando como un loco en los ratos que no esté dejándome la piel en el trabajo. Supongo que, si se concibe una tipografía excelente, no importa que salga a la luz ahora o dentro de diez años. Entre tanto, seguiré anotando mis nuevas ideas y emplearé este año en descartar las malas y disfrutar de las excelentes tipografías que existen en el mercado.

Lopetz – Büro Destruct

Büro Destruct lleva en la vanguardia del diseño gráfico suizo desde mediados de la década de

1990. Su trabajo ha influenciado a diseñadores de todo el planeta, gracias a dos libros publicados por Die Gestalten Verlag. Desde sus albores, el estudio ha creado tipografías con un estilo original y ha decidido compartir una parte sustancial de ellas con otros diseñadores de forma gratuita.

Cuando empezaste a crear las primeras tipografías de Büro Destruct para utilizarlas en tu propio trabajo, inmediatamente las pusiste a disposición del público, y sigues haciéndolo...
L: El diseño tipográfico siempre ha sido una parte importante de nuestra concepción de la profesión. La razón principal para crear tipografías personalizadas es expresarnos con un lenguaje único en nuestro trabajo de diseño gráfico cotidiano. La segunda razón es dar a conocer esas tipografías y, de ese modo, compartir nuestros diseños tipográficos con otros diseñadores.

¿Cómo decidís qué tipografías sacáis al mercado de forma gratuita y cuáles como tipos comerciales?
L: Depende de la cantidad de trabajo que hayamos invertido en la creación de la tipografía. En su mayoría, las familias gratuitas no nos han robado mucho tiempo. Cuanto más «profesional» queremos hacer una tipografía (trabajando el kerning, los diversos estilos y la legibilidad), más posibilidades hay de que sea de pago. También tenemos en cuenta la utilidad final de la tipografía. Si pensamos que una empresa importante con un presupuesto enorme podría utilizar una fuente con fines comerciales y publicitarios, la incorporamos en la gama de tipografías de pago.

Sois un estudio de diseño gráfico reputado. ¿Creéis que eso ayuda a que otros diseñadores se tomen vuestras tipografías gratuitas más en serio?
L: Sin duda alguna, nuestra reputación nos ayuda a promocionar tanto las tipografías gratuitas como las de pago. Pero nosotros lo vemos en el sentido

inverso: nuestras tipografías han contribuido a que nos convirtamos en un «estudio de diseño gráfico reputado». En comparación con otros diseñadores tipográficos, nuestras fuentes pueden considerarse menos serias, pero eso forma parte de la forma en que trabajamos con ellas. Nuestro objetivo no es crear una nueva Helvetica, Garamond o lo que sea, puesto que tardaríamos años en hacerlo. Lo que nosotros pretendemos es concebir nuevas formas gráficas que puedan recopilarse en un alfabeto y distribuirlas. Así fue como empezamos a crear tipografías en los primeros años de Büro Destruct, en 1995. La familia Flossy, por ejemplo, fue nuestro primer diseño tipográfico: no era más que una colección de posiciones diversas de un carácter en forma de oveja.

¿Podrías explicarme la metodología que aplicáis para diseñar una tipografía? ¿Se os ocurre primero una idea para una tipografía o más bien tenéis una idea para un proyecto de diseño y pensáis que os convendría contar con una fuente nueva?
L: Normalmente, todas las tipografías de Büro Destruct nacen tras la creación de un logotipo, un título para un póster de un concierto, un *flyer* para una fiesta o una carátula de un CD. El mejor ejemplo es la tipografía BD Balduin, que en un principio concebimos para el logotipo del artista musical Balduin. A veces generamos una tipografía a partir de una forma simple que nos apetece explorar en un alfabeto completo. Una fuente de inspiración magnífica es viajar a países donde se hablen idiomas con alfabetos no latinos, como Japón, el mundo árabe, etc. No sabemos leerlos, así que nos limitamos a observar las formas y reutilizarlas en nuestros alfabetos.

¿Soléis reutilizar vuestras tipografías existentes para vuestros trabajos de diseño?
L: Nuestra política es incorporar las tipografías cuando tiene lógica, puesto que responden a nuestro propio lenguaje, pero habitualmente acabamos

por utilizar fuentes nuevas. Una razón importante para hacerlo es que solemos crear tipografías vinculadas a un proyecto o una fuente determinados. Pertenecen a ese proyecto o periodo. Compartimos con otros diseñadores las nuevas tipografías que confeccionamos y lo que más nos sorprende es comprobar cómo ellos aplican nuestras letras a su propio contexto.

Shamrock

Shamrock (alias Jeroen Klaver) es conocido principalmente por sus preciosas ilustraciones de estética retro. Pocas personas saben que posee una titulación en diseño gráfico y que ha creado tipografías tanto gratuitas como de pago. Muchas de sus fuentes evocan la atmósfera de su estilo de dibujo, porque la mayoría las concibe para trabajar con sus ilustraciones. De hecho, si se utiliza una de sus tipografías, uno acaba imbuyendo a su diseño de parte del espíritu artístico de Klaver: un estilo divertido, animado e irresistible.

Conocía tus ilustraciones, pero la verdad es que no conocía bien tus tipografías. ¿Qué lugar ocupa la tipografía en tu trabajo?
S: Un lugar importante. Empecé a trabajar como diseñador gráfico porque siempre me ha encantado hacer cosas como revistas, fanzines y *flyers*. No soy la clase de diseñador que encarga una imagen, inserta un poco de texto encima y la envía. Me gusta que mi trabajo destile sensación de conjunto. Todo tiene que estar bien hecho y responder a un equilibrio. Tengo muy en cuenta el texto; he rechazado encargos porque la redacción carecía de sentido. Cuando uno lo hace todo por sí mismo, puede hacer lo que quiera. Además, siempre siento curiosidad por cómo se hacen las cosas. Sé que siempre hay personas que pueden hacerlo todo

mucho mejor que yo, pero probar a hacer cosas nuevas por mí mismo me infunde respeto hacia esas personas y me permite comunicarme más fácilmente con ellas.

Empecé a dibujar letras en serio en el instituto. Dedico un montón de tiempo a hacerlo y me gustaría poderle dedicar incluso más, pero no me ayuda a pagar las facturas. En términos económicos, por consiguiente, mis tipografías no ocupan ningún lugar en mi trabajo, pero son una gran parte de quien creo que soy.

Salvo por las tipografías Elvis, todas tus creaciones se distribuyen de forma gratuita. ¿Existe alguna razón concreta para ello?
S: No todas las tipografías son gratuitas. Tengo más «tipografías comerciales» casi acabadas, pero nunca encuentro el tiempo para ultimarlas y lanzarlas al mercado como es debido. Llevo años diciendo: «el verano que viene (o el invierno, cuando es verano), me tomaré unos cuantos meses de vacaciones para poner mis asuntos en orden». Pero nunca logro hacerlo. Muchas de las fuentes gratuitas no son más que experimentos pésimos que no podría vender con la cabeza alta. Incluso hay algunas muestras viejas trazadas entre ellas. Todas son fuentes que he creado en algún momento para un trabajo de diseño y después he decidido colgarlas en mi sitio web. Realmente solo me dejé la piel en unas pocas de ellas, y me gustaría tener más tiempo para convertirlas en algo que merezca la pena. No soy un defensor de las fuentes gratuitas per se. De hecho, creo que el mundo está plagado de diseños feos realizados por gente que no sabe diseñar y que piensa que basta con saber manejar un ordenador. Lo único que hace esta gente es limitarse a coger unas cuantas cosas de Internet y hacer un pastiche con ellas. No me importa que lo hagan, me alegro de que se diviertan, pero el aspecto negativo es que muchos clientes empiezan a convencerse de que así es como funciona el diseño gráfico. Por otro lado, hacer regalos atrae a visitantes, y eso puede acabar redundando en forjarse una reputación o en obtener nuevos clientes. También te puede poner en contacto con colegas o músicos que utilizan una tipografía para un CD y luego te envían un ejemplar del disco. ¡Estupendo!

¿También diseñas tipografías sin tener una aplicación en mente o las creas en función de tus necesidades como diseñador/ilustrador?
S: Sí lo hago, pero esas tipografías no las distribuyo de manera gratuita. Diseñar una tipografía conlleva mucho trabajo y utilizar tipos personales puede otorgar a un diseñador un cierto grado de exclusividad. Preferiría ver mis fuentes utilizadas de un modo bonito a usadas en exceso, pero estoy demasiado ocupado para empezar a vender mis tipografías como debería. Prefiero que la creación de tipografías siga siendo algo que me encanta hacer, en lugar de convertirlo en una profesión que me dé dolores de cabeza. A veces, cuando diseño un folleto, un librillo o algo por el estilo, me resulta más sencillo crear una fuente con unos cuantos caracteres (o escanear algunas muestras antiguas y convertirlas en una) que explorar todo mi catálogo en busca de la idónea. Y muchas de esas fuentes sí las distribuyo de manera gratuita.

¿Creas tus fuentes desde el punto de vista de un diseñador gráfico o de un ilustrador?
S: Mis «tipografías comerciales» son más personales, más en la línea de mi trabajo de ilustración. Intento que las curvas, la sensación y el movimiento me complazcan tanto como en mis ilustraciones y mis animaciones. Es algo que nadie me pide que haga, a diferencia de lo que ocurre en mis trabajos de diseño, en los que uno crea en función de las exigencias del cliente; a veces he tenido que asesorar en contra de los designios de mi cliente. Creo que el arte se sitúa en un extremo del espectro, el diseño en el otro y la ilustración se encuentra exactamente en el punto medio.

Responde a un montón de decisiones personales y, sin embargo, se supone que debe contar la historia del cliente. Por otro lado, diseñar tipografías ha influido sobremanera en mi trabajo como ilustrador. Trabajo de una forma demasiado limpia. Todas mis curvas son más precisas de lo necesario. En una ilustración, no pasa nada, pero cuando hago una animación esto me roba mucho tiempo. Lo que ocurre es que no puedo resistirme a la tentación de corregir una curva en un dibujo, ¡aunque solo se vea durante una fracción de segundo!

Index

Index of extended character sets

As is the nature of free fonts, the character sets of the fonts in this book are not uniform. Most (but not all) of the fonts contain at least a full set of upper and lower case letters and numbers; many contain accented characters used in Western European languages. We have also included a few exceptional fonts which contain extended character sets; these include accented Latin characters used in Eastern European languages and/or Cyrillic or Greek characters. The following is a list of fonts containing some or all characters in these extended character sets.

Index des séries de caractères additionnels

De par la nature même des fontes libres, les séries de caractères des fontes de ce livre ne sont pas uniformes. La plupart des fontes (mais pas toutes) possèdent au moins une série complète de lettres capitales, de minuscules et de chiffres. Beaucoup possèdent les caractères accentués utilisés dans les langues d'Europe occidentale. Nous avons aussi ajouté quelques fontes exceptionnelles avec des séries de caractères additionnels : celles-ci contiennent les caractères romains accentués utilisés dans les langues d'Europe orientale et/ou les caractères cyrilliques ou grecs. Vous trouverez ci-après une liste des fontes contenant une partie ou la totalité des caractères appartenant à ces séries de caractères additionnels.

Index der erweiterten Zeichensätze

Wie gewöhnlich bei kostenlosen Fonts sind die Zeichensätze der Schriften in diesem Buch nicht uniform. Die meisten (aber nicht alle) der Schriften enthalten mindestens einen vollständigen Satz von Groß- und Kleinbuchstaben und Ziffern; viele enthalten die akzentuierten Zeichen, die in westeuropäischen Sprachen verwendet werden. Wir haben ebenfalls eine Reihe von außergewöhnlichen Fonts aufgenommen, die erweiterte Zeichensätze enthalten; diese umfassen akzentuierte Zeichen des lateinischen Alphabets, die in osteuropäischen Sprachen verwendet werden bzw. kyrillische oder griechische Zeichen. Auf der nächsten Seite folgt eine Liste der Fonts, die einige oder sämtliche Zeichen in diesen erweiterten Zeichensätzen enthalten.

Índice de juegos de caracteres ampliados

Como es habitual en las fuentes gratuitas, los juegos de caracteres de las familias suministradas en este libro no son uniformes. La mayoría de ellas, aunque no todas, contienen al menos un juego completo de letras mayúsculas y minúsculas y números; muchas incorporan además los caracteres acentuados propios de los idiomas de la Europa occidental. También hemos incluido unas cuantas fuentes excepcionales con juegos de caracteres ampliados, es decir, con los caracteres latinos acentuados propios de las lenguas de la Europa del Este y/o caracteres griegos o cirílicos. A continuación se relacionan las que contienen algunos o todos los caracteres de estos juegos ampliados.

Central and Eastern European

Astigmatic	Haunt	39
exljbris	Anivers	82
	Diavlo	84
Grixel	Acme	118
	Kyrou	120
GUST	Antykwa Półtawskiego	124
Igino Marini	Double Pica Pro	128
	DW Pica Pro	128
	English Pro	129
	French Canon Pro	131
	Great Primer Pro	132
Janusz Nowacki	Antykwa Torunska	134
	Cyklop	138
	Kurier	139
Larabie	Berylium	150
	Credit Valley	151
	Kirsty	156
Objets Dart	Enigmatic (Unicode)	194
	Hindsight (Unicode)	195
Reading Type	Bentham	214
Typedifferent	BD Spacy 125	247
Typodermic	Expressway	250
	Gnuolane	251
	Mufferaw	251
	Nasalization	252
	Negotiate	252
	Octin College	253
	Octin Prison	253
	Octin Sports	253
	Octin Spraypaint	255
	Octin Stencil	255
	Octin Vintage	255

Cyrillic

Janusz Nowacki	Antykwa Torunska	134
	Kurier	139
Objets Dart	Enigmatic (Unicode)	194
	Hindsight (Unicode)	195
	Intruder	197
Typodermic	Expressway	250

Greek

Grixel	Acme	118
	Kyrou	120
Janusz Nowacki	Antykwa Torunska	134
	Kurier	139
Objets Dart	Enigmatic (Unicode)	194
	Hindsight (Unicode)	195

Katakana (Japanese)

Flat-it	Sushitaro	110
Typedifferent	BD Eject ktna	243
	BD Relaunch ktna	246
	BD Wakarimasu ktna	248

Armenian, Hebrew & Cherokee

Objets Dart	Hindsight (Unicode)	195